How to Talk to Anyone About Anything

Make Real Friends and Improve Your Social Skills by Mastering Small Talk and Making Easy Connections
(2022 Guide for Beginners)

Daisy Byrd

Contents

INTRODUCTION 7
First and foremost, your social connection is everything. 11
The Starting Point 15
Chapter 1 17
It All Begins with You 17
Developing Your Self-Concept 22
Your Sense of Self is Created 26
Decide on Your Values 27
Having Enough You Time 29
If Assistance Is Required, Seek It 30
The Synopsis 31
Chapter 2 32
It All Begins with Listening 32
There Are Two Kinds of Listening 34
How to Listen in Order to Understand 36
The Synopsis 40
Chapter 3 42
Improving Your Listening Skills 42
Reduce Distractions 42
Be Devoid of Judgments 44
Pose the Correct Questions 44
The Synopsis 45
Chapter 4 46
It's All About Questions 46

The Influence of Questions 47
Using Questions to Begin Conversations 50
Getting to Know Someone New (Networking, social event, etc.) 52
Tell me a little bit about yourself. 52
What was the highlight of your week? 52
Are you currently working on anything exciting? 53
Have you visited this location before? 53
Questions to Ask on a First Date 54
Fun, Personal Small-Talk Questions to Ask Anyone, Anywhere 55
How to Ask the Right Questions 56
Locate the Line 56
Consider the Social Hierarchy. 57
Keep Your Inquiries Open-Ended 58
The Synopsis 59
Chapter 5 60
How to Have a Conversation with Anyone 60
Step One - Make a Good First Impression 61
Examining the Situation 62
Creating a Room 66
Step 2: Make Your First Move 68
Step Three - Locate the Link 72
The Art of Mirroring 74
Step Four - Dealing with Potential Obstacles 76
Chapter 6 80
Mastering the Art of Small Talk 80

The Fundamentals of Small Talk 81
The Influence of Enthusiasm 82
Finding Interesting Small-Talk Topics 86
You'll Have to Carry the Conversation... Initially 89
Meaningful relationships take time to develop. 90
Topics to Avoid in Small Talk 94
Religion 94
Politics 95
The end of life 95
Sexing 95
Health and happiness 96
Personal life slander 96
Inappropriate jokes 96
Physical Appearance 97
Ex-partners or friendships 97
Are there any restricted conversation topics? 97
Putting the Conversation to Rest 98
Developing the Art of Small Talk 99
The Synopsis 102
Chapter 7 103
Intricate Ways to Be More Charismatic 103
The Synopsis 111
Chapter 8 112
How to Be More Confident 112
Overcome Self-Sabotaging Thoughts 115
A Quick Little Test 116

Use Self-Assured Body Language 118
Get Your Hands On 119
Implement Make Eye Contact 120
Reduce your speed. 121
The Synopsis 122
Chapter 9 123
How to Tell Stories That Stick 123
You're one of them. 124
Locating the Assailant Plotline 125
Creating a Story Collection 127
What is the Best Way to Tell a Story? 130
Think about the Length 131
Choosing the Correct Particulars 131
Adding to Your Stories 133
The Synopsis 138
Chapter 10 139
Becoming an Interesting Person 139
More Books to Read 141
Change Up Your Routine 142
Contribute Your Time 143
Accept Your Fear 144
Use Your Time Wisely 144
Have Interesting Discussions 145
Attempt New Hobbies 146
The Synopsis 147
ChapterEleven – Creating Meaningful Relationships . 147

The Advantages are Unrivaled 149
Understanding the Obstacles 150
You Can't Be Friends With Everyone 151
Spend Time with Your New Companions 152
Support One Another 153
Be True to Yourself 154
The Synopsis 155
Last Thoughts 156

INTRODUCTION

Not long ago, my friend Kyle approached me and told me about a recent weekend in which he had attended his sister's wedding. Kyle had been married for nearly twenty years before his divorce a few months before, and this wedding was one of his first "outings" by himself.

He told me about the big day over a beer. At ten, he was surrounded by friends and family, people he saw nearly every week or texted every now and then. The ceremony was lovely. Everyone was content. They took taxis from the church to the reception, which was held at a large fancy downtown hotel.

Kyle was busy making sure everything was running smoothly behind the scenes when he arrived.

People ate food, drank, started dancing, and generally had a good time in true wedding fashion.

Relatives from both sides of the new family gathered to commemorate this joyous occasion.

But it wasn't all smiles, booze, and confetti for Kyle.

Plunged into the vast depths beyond his comfort zone, he told me that as soon as he began interacting with strangers, friends of friends, and distant relatives, he realized he had no idea how to talk to any of them.

He recalled an embarrassing incident in which his sister's new husband's cousin came over and said, "Hey," and he froze, literally not saying anything. The word "awkward" was an understatement.

Kyle was stuck after the obligatory "How are you?" and "Isn't it a beautiful service, right?" His mind began to race with worry. He was bombarded with innumerable thoughts, such as, "What should I say?" What can I do to make this person laugh? Do they give a damn what I have to say? Who is this individual? What are their passions? and so forth.

Outside of his mind, and back in reality, this all came out as generic small talk, awkward silences, and uncertain glances at the floor.

"Oh my God, it was horrible. Kathy (Kyle's ex-wife) was a captivating individual, but I had no idea how much she carried our conversations while we were married. I have the impression that I am unable to communicate with anyone. What are you talking about? Are people interested in what I have to say? Even if they did, I don't think I'd be brave enough to try. "Lord knows when or if I'll ever start dating again."

As we finished our drinks and paid the bill, I told him that becoming confident, or even just speaking to other people, isn't some far-fetched idea reserved for only the most extroverted people who exude natural charisma. Oh, no!

I was like Kyle over a decade ago, and then for the majority of my life. I was awkward, shy, and withdrawn throughout school, college, university, and a smattering of first and part-time jobs, eventually leading to the start of my career.

I was the guy who sat in the middle of the class because I wasn't cool enough to sit in the back or smart enough to sit in the front. I was the one who went unnoticed.

I had some friends I'd known my entire life, but the older I got, the more socially anxious I became, and the more isolated I became. It was incapacitating. Since I was a child, I hadn't pushed myself to talk to anyone or taken risks when meeting new people. It was as if I'd forgotten how to do it after all these years.

It was difficult to meet new people. It was impossible for me to date.

Speaking with customers in my part-time jobs was a mess, and selling to clients in my career was, at best, untrustworthy. I could only occasionally talk to someone without breaking out in a cold sweat or feeling like I was about to have a panic attack. I had good days and bad days, but as the years passed, I came to two major realizations that eventually led to me changing my life.

First and foremost, your social connection is everything.

Your ability to communicate and connect influences your relationships with others, your job, yourself, and your overall happiness and life satisfaction. You could have millions of dollars in the bank and everything that a successful person has, but if you're lonely, you're unhappy.

You can be poor and have nothing materially, but if you're surrounded by caring people with whom you have a meaningful connection, you can feel like the wealthiest person on the planet.

My second realization was equally life-altering.

Being self-assured, charismatic, and open to connecting with others is not a natural trait. I used to think that confident people, those who could hold an entire audience or keep you hooked on their every word, had a natural talent for confidence. I was mistaken.

Confidence and charisma are learned, honed, and practiced skills. They are even teachable.

Have you ever walked into a room and noticed that one person who dominates the conversation, perhaps in a group of friends or at a work meeting? Perhaps you have a friend who can seem to talk to anyone about anything, and no matter what the situation, they seem to carry the flow of the conversation effortlessly? Have you ever felt envious of someone?

This isn't the first time that person has done something like this. You can see years of practice. Several years of trial and error. Years of making mistakes, trying new techniques, and learning from each experience. They would have had awkward moments in school, as well as embarrassing meetings and conversations where nothing seemed to work.

And all of this begs more questions.

What can you do differently?

How do you gain self-assurance?

How are you supposed to talk to anyone about anything?

I've always been the quiet one. I spent the majority of my life as him. I was afraid to share my thoughts, and now I'm writing books you're reading (which still amazes me!). I'm capable of dating and holding my own. I am capable of presenting meetings and engaging everyone in the room. I can tell stories to groups of friends and have them hang on every word I say. Not long ago, I gave a talk to a public speaking group, and a member of the audience approached me and said it was one of the best talks they had seen in years.

I don't say that to brag. I know I have a long way to go compared to the greats, but seeing my own journey from being the awkward kid to speaking in front of a group of 30 people warmed my heart. If it's possible for me, it's certainly possible for anyone.

Finally, a few questions.

How do you improve your swimming?

You spend a lot of time in the pool.

How do you improve your writing skills? You are a writer.

How do you improve your ability to connect with others? You make connections with people.

Confidence, like all life skills, is something that must be practiced and honed over time, but just as an athlete needs a coach, I'm writing this book to help guide you along the path of your own journey. First, we'll go over your mindset and get it in order so you're actually ready to meet new people.

Then we'll get into the meat of this book. This is where I'll talk about how to strike up a conversation with someone, find people who share your interests, and use questions to guide the conversation. You'll also learn how to be more charismatic and confident and how to act and present yourself in any situation.

This book aims to be the key that opens so many doors in your life through connection and opportunities, so let's not linger any longer.

The Starting Point

When it comes to making a change in your life, these are the three most important factors to consider:

Education.Awareness.Practice.

You'll need knowledge and information to make the best decisions possible. You need awareness to put everything you've learned into practice, to recognize where you go wrong, what you do right, and where you need to improve.

Finally, you must continue to practice and improve your skills.

I've been on this journey before.

I was unfulfilled and dissatisfied with my life in my mid-20s. I was living in a big city with no one I could truly call a close friend. There is no partner. It should have been an exciting time, as I was starting a new career with promising prospects, but I held myself back. I was ticking the creative boxes, but I wasn't a people person, and people are the ones who give opportunities.

I made the decision that I needed to make a change.

I received an education. I read research papers, scientific papers, articles, and research reports. I listened to podcasts and read books. I applied all of this knowledge in my own life, being conscious of what I was doing so that I could judge for myself what was right and wrong. I figured out what works for me, practiced it, and used these experiences to propel myself to where I am now.

What's the best part about it all?

It works fantastically well.

Using my own experiences, scientific studies, and a plethora of research, I've compiled this book to be essentially everything you'll need to know when learning how to communicate with others.

So, as we get into the meat of this book, I want you to keep an open mind. Be eager to learn and absorb what you read. I strongly advise getting a pen and notebook to jot down ideas, techniques, and communication strategies that resonate with you, as this will improve your ability to absorb them.

It's finally time.

Chapter 1

It All Begins with You

"You can always change and become a better version of yourself, no matter who you are, what you've done, or where you've come from." -Madonna

When you first picked up this book, you probably read the title and imagined what it would be like to have the ability to communicate with anyone. Maybe you fantasize about telling stories around the water cooler, with everyone staring in awe at how good your stories are.

Perhaps it's the same in your dating life, and you yearn to be the charismatic boy or girl who enchants everyone who listens to you. Perhaps you want to improve your communication skills with coworkers, managers, bosses, or clients.

Yikes! I'm sure you're beginning to see how much communicating with others affects every aspect of your life! However, I want you to set aside your fantasies for the time being (I promise we'll make them a reality later) because we need to start with you.

Yup. It's time to take a long, hard look in the mirror at ourselves because guess what? There's a reason why people say, "You can't properly love other people until you learn to love yourself first." It may sound philosophical and like something you've heard before, but bear with me.

We're going to put this into action.

Let's start with the fundamentals of who you are right now.

Your sense of self must be defined because it will literally dictate how you act in every single situation from now on, and you can either allow this to happen unconsciously or be aware and in control of it. Don't worry; everything will make sense as we go.

To get your creative juices flowing, here's a question: Who are you?

Simply consider and be aware of whatever thoughts arise.

Now, take those thoughts and discard any basic identity information, such as your name, age, or job. How do you see yourself now? What type of person do you associate with? What are your beliefs and values? Yes, we're diving right into the deep end.

When I was 23, and my self-development was just getting started, I remember journaling one night for what must have been the first time in my life (I had just watched a YouTube video about how life-changing it can be), and I asked myself these very questions.

Surprisingly, I had no responses. What did I have faith in? What did I hold dear? What exactly was I? Murdering people, in my opinion, is wrong. Gravity, I believe, exists. Fast food, in my opinion, should be consumed in moderation. As you can see, I was scraping the bottom of the barrel for ideas and didn't have a comprehensive answer. I realized I lacked a sense of self.

Everything revolves around your sense of self. It defines who you are.

In psychology, a sense of self is an all-encompassing view of oneself, beliefs, purpose in this world, and identity. What do you think? How can you expect to be yourself in the presence of others if you don't know your own sense of self?

A strong sense of self motivates you to get out of bed in the morning because you are fully aware of your life's mission and the causes you are fighting for. You understand where you stand and what is important to you. That is not to say that your sense of self cannot and will not change over time. In fact, if it does not change, this can be unhealthy, also known as being set in your ways. Having a sense of self, on the other hand, is critical. You can't be confident unless you have it.

Erika Myers, an Oregon-based professional counselor, puts it succinctly.

"Having a strong sense of self is extremely helpful in making life decisions." Knowing what comes from our own self versus what comes from others allows us to live authentically, from something as simple as favorite foods to larger issues like personal values."

Genuine living. Isn't that the ideal situation? No, this is not a dream. It's a requirement.

When you can learn to be yourself authentically with yourself, you can begin to be yourself authentically with others. Do you know how they say that you can only truly love others once you learn to love yourself? We're playing on the same field as that ideology.

Being authentically you means you recognize that you are not perfect (and that no one is), but you are willing to accept your flaws while also embracing your strengths because they define you more than anything else.

A lack of self-esteem is a problem.

You'll find yourself drifting through life if you don't know who you are or what you stand for. You will be unsure and indecisive. Your life will be devoid of momentum and drive. You'll be anxious and dissatisfied, but you won't be able to pinpoint why because you don't know what you want and don't want.

Remember when I was at Kyle's sister's wedding? His marriage had given him his entire sense of self in many ways, and he didn't know who he was without it. He was drowsy while conversing with others at the wedding.

Was he just looking for a good time? To simply put on a brave face and show his support for his sister? Was he there to make new friends? Was he looking to date or even hook up with someone new?

None of these things are inherently good or bad because they are determined by the individual and their wants or needs. However, without understanding what these wants or needs are, nothing can be done to address them, and thus the anxiety cycle continues.

Developing Your Self-Concept

To reiterate, you cannot have relationships with others until you first learn to have relationships with yourself, which brings us nicely to your first exercise in this book. Don't be concerned. While it may appear to be a daunting task, we will break it down and work through it together. I've got you covered.

Take a pen and paper and write the phrase "Checking in with Myself." As the name implies, we're going to check in and discover who you are right now.

Make sure you're in a quiet place where you can be alone with your thoughts.

According to Healthline.com, your sense of self will fall somewhere on a spectrum, according to Healthline.com. Either you have a strong, complete sense of self, or you are somewhere in the middle. Let's find out where you are.

Pose some of these questions to yourself and jot down whatever comes to mind. Also, I know what it's like to read books like this, and it's easy to just skim over these action points and do them in your head. If you want real change in your life (which I'm assuming is why you picked up this book in the first place), then do this activity and see what happens.

How can you expect anything to change if you don't take the initiative to try something new? Anyway, I wish someone had told me that years ago. Let's get started with the questions!

- What type of person do you aspire to be?
- What kind of person are you at the moment?
- What words would you use to describe yourself?
- Do you believe you've evolved significantly over the years?
- What are your strengths in life?
- What areas of your life do you struggle with?
- What do you care deeply about loving?
- What do you care deeply about hating?
- What kinds of relationships do you have in your life?
- What types of relationships do you desire in your life?
- How much control do you feel over your life?

You don't have to answer all of these questions, but if you look at one and think it's a little difficult, I recommend devoting a little more time to it because that's where you'll find the interesting answers. Try to be as truthful as possible.

Be aware that many of your responses will be influenced by how you perceive yourself as an individual as well as how others have told you they perceive you. For example, if your partner constantly refers to you as lazy, you may begin to believe you are, even if you know deep down that you are not. This is one of the ways to develop a false sense of self. This process is all about discovering your true sense of self, rather than what other people and their perspectives have imposed on you.

The same is true in social groups, whether at school, with friends, with family, or at work. You may act a certain way to fit in, but you are not the person you are portraying.

Try to cut through these myths and write down who you truly believe you are, for better or worse.

When you're finished, take some time to go over your answers again.

Were you surprised by what you wrote? Did anything come to mind that you hadn't thought about in a long time? Did you anticipate some of the responses? Did you experience a brief flashback to a "past you" that you had forgotten about or thought was lost? Good. Whatever came up, clarity is on its way.

Perhaps a few days or a week, take some time to process what you wrote down. New ideas may come to you as you think about this whole concept (add them to your existing answers), and you may change your mind or have more certainty about other points you write down.

At the end of the week, go over everything again and move on to the next step.

Your Sense of Self is Created

You can be reborn as the true you, like a phoenix from the ashes with this knowledge.

This is not a one-time event but rather a continuous process that evolves into a lifelong journey. Your sense of self will change and adapt as you have new experiences and learn new things, which is wonderful. What we're doing now is laying the groundwork for future growth.

I recall going through this process and being astounded by how passive I was in my life. I adopted a different persona with family, friends, and coworkers, attempting to be who I thought these other people wanted me to be rather than simply being myself. I was constantly anxious, afraid of being judged and rejected, and suppressing my true self. I desired freedom, and this is how I obtained it.

Decide on Your Values

Did you make a note of how much you adore animals or your desire to save the planet? If this is the case, it's time to start choosing cruelty-free brands and spending time learning more about the food you eat and the clothes you wear.

Did you make a list of how much you value your health and taking care of yourself? It's time to start exercising and eating right.

Do you value other people's relationships and experiences? It's time to call your mother and make plans with your friends.

Do you place a premium on genuine people and open relationships? It's time to think about what you're going to do about that toxic friend you've been avoiding.

Using the information you learned about yourself in the previous section, you should be able to establish at least some values in your life that you believe in, allowing you to make choices in your life that you actually want to make. Making these choices will provide you with life satisfaction and a sense of self.

Furthermore, you can learn to eliminate things that are unimportant to you and do not serve your beliefs and values. I value connected relationships, but I was lonely and didn't feel like they were meeting my needs, so I filled the void with video games.

While I enjoyed computer games on occasion, I didn't enjoy playing them for six hours a day to keep myself from feeling lonely, so I limited my gaming to two hours on weekends and spent the extra time on my relationships. By making the right decisions, I was able to find balance in my life naturally.

Decide on your priorities. Find out what is important to you. Make the right decisions. This action will give you a sense of self.

Having Enough You Time

The only way to figure out what matters to you is to spend enough time alone with yourself, listening to your thoughts and processing how you're feeling. It's so easy to numb out a bad day with TV, Netflix, and social media, but how will you learn about yourself if you don't think about it?

There are numerous ways to accomplish this, whether you enjoy reading or listening to music or prefer more hands-on self-help techniques such as journaling and meditation. It's entirely up to you, and if you're unsure, try a variety of approaches to see what works best for you as an individual.

If Assistance Is Required, Seek It

The last thing I want you to remember is that your self-help journey does not have to be a lonely one. If someone you cared about was going through this experience, it's safe to say that if they needed assistance or support, you'd do whatever you could to help.

The same is true for you. People will always be willing to assist you, especially if they are a loved one, but they must first know that you want the assistance.

Assume you're dealing with something you can't seem to overcome, such as a mental health condition like depression or anxiety (both of which are very common in people who lack a sense of self). In that case, professional assistance is always available.

The Synopsis

That brings us to the end of the first chapter. Is the journey so far what you expected? Didn't we go a little deep? It's all right. It's all-important, and what's amazing is that by focusing solely on developing your sense of self, you'll notice real changes in your life and relationships with others almost immediately.

You will naturally be more confident in yourself because you know yourself. Because you know what you believe in, you can share your thoughts with others and begin to have more in-depth meaningful discussions.

To summarize, you must first focus on developing your sense of self by: defining your values and beliefs; spending time getting to know yourself; and understanding what makes you, you.

As I previously stated, this is just the foundation for becoming better at small talk, and if you want to delve deeper, you are welcome to do so. However, in our journey together, we'll re-evaluate how to talk to anyone, beginning with one of the most critical skills you'll need to know.

Chapter 2

It All Begins with Listening

"When you speak, all you are doing is repeating what you already know." But if you pay attention, you might learn something new." — The Dalai Lama

You probably saw this coming. Every relationship you have, have had, and will have for the rest of your life is built on effective communication. The ability to listen to others communicating with you is the most important aspect of this.

Listening is important because you're giving someone your full attention, which allows you to understand what they're saying, which is the best foundation for a genuine relationship. Everyone wishes to be heard and understood by others.

According to a 2015 study conducted by Michigan State University, active listening (listening with intent) will allow you to communicate more clearly and concisely with others and better understand the world.

As a result, listening not only improves your own speaking abilities but also allows you to connect with those around you. Consider talking to someone who clearly isn't paying attention to you. You've been there, haven't you? It's awful, and you don't want to be around that person for very long. Let's look at how you can improve your listening skills.

There Are Two Kinds of Listening

Listening. You have a conversation, listen to what the other person says, and respond to what they say, correct? That's a discussion.

Relationships are formed as a result of this. Right? It's all very simple. No, not entirely.

According to research, there are 18 different types of listening, including states such as biased listening, inactive listening, deep listening, empathetic listening, comprehensive listening, and so on. Still, for the sake of simplicity, I'd like to divide it into two categories.

- **Listening to comprehend**
- **Listening to respond**

When you speak to the vast majority of people, they will listen in order to respond. This essentially means that, rather than listening to someone, this person already knows what point they want to make next, and they are simply waiting for the other person to finish speaking so they can have their turn.

When I first started dating my partner, we visited her parents for the weekend, which was a great example of this. After reading about all the health benefits, my partner decided to try a vegan diet and couldn't bear the thought of eating an animal.

When she told her father, he asked, "Why do you want to do that?" Meat is delicious. You're aware that you'll never be able to eat burgers again?"

"Or a delicious steak!" her mother added.

"Well, the impact of the meat industry on the rest of the planet is just not something I want on my conscience, and don't even get me started on how poorly the living creatures are treated," my partner tried to explain.

"I couldn't do it," he responded. "I just have an unhealthy obsession with steak."

Had my partner been heard? No. Even though her father is a nice guy, he believes that meat is good and that nothing can stop it. No matter what my partner said, he would have maintained his position that meat is amazing and the best thing ever.

They are listening in order to respond. To have a more progressive conversation, he could have asked, "Why?" What are the health advantages? "What effect does animal agriculture have on the environment?"

And if he had listened to her and still didn't mind eating meat, he would have at least listened and given it a chance. By simply listening to her response, they passed up an opportunity to understand their daughter on an individual level.

The best, most meaningful conversations are built on everyone's goal of understanding each other and sharing the facts and why people think and feel the way they do. Taking this approach allows you to understand others as individuals rather than imposing your own narrative on them.

How to Listen in Order to Understand

This is the logical next question. So, how do you listen in order to understand?

The same MSU study discovered, as with most confidence and communication techniques, that listening to understand is a skill that can be learned and practiced, and to quote the report directly: "Active listening requires time and practice." It does, however, become easier with each use of active listening. It can assist you in navigating difficult conversations. More than that, it promotes better overall communication, understanding, and, ultimately, better relationships with family, friends, and coworkers."

Because practice makes perfect, here are the skills for actionable listening to understand.

- **Give Your Complete Attention**

This may seem obvious, but be honest with yourself: how often do you listen to someone and then clock out, perhaps thinking about what you should do next, what's on TV later, or how you're going to respond? This is not giving someone your undivided attention.

You can accomplish this by minimizing distractions, such as not playing with your phone or watching TV, making eye contact with someone, facing the person you're speaking to; not multi-tasking, and bringing yourself back to the present moment when you find yourself drifting.

Concentrating on the center of your palm is a great trick I learned to help you maintain focus. You can do it right now, and you'll notice how your focus shifts to the center of your hand. See how it causes your thoughts to stop and how much more focused you become? Experiment with it in your conversations to see how effective it is.

I know this all sounds like common sense, but it is easy to forget and fall into bad habits because it is. A Harvard study conducted in 1957 even used these same techniques to help people listen, resulting in a 40% increase in people's listening abilities, so try it for yourself!

- **Listen to what the other person has to say.**

When someone is talking to you, it's all too easy to get into the habit of interrupting, which is a bad habit. It also implies that you're not listening to understand the person; rather, you're listening to make your own points, which is not the foundation for a meaningful conversation. You can help not interrupt people by doing the following: minimizing distractions, such as not answering the phone; letting go of your point and responding to what the other person is saying; waiting until they have finished speaking; and asking a question if you need more clarity on what they said, rather than simply going back to your original point.

This is an important technique to consider because interrupting is a missed opportunity to understand the other person, but it also sends the message that you don't respect the other person enough or believe that their opinions aren't worth listening to, and that whatever you're interrupting them with is more important than them.

This will not reflect well on you.

- **Listen with your body.**

Along with improving your listening skills, being aware of your body and how you control it can be a great way to improve your attentiveness. While I already mentioned making eye contact, you can also do the following: Turning your body to face the person speaking, Nodding occasionally, Smiling, but not too much (don't want them to think you're weird) Saying "uh-huh" to show you're engaged in the conversation and want them to continue

- **Adopt an open posture and repeat their points back to them for clarity.**

The repetition of a point is always mentioned as one of the most popular ways to improve a conversation. If someone says, "I like chocolate because it's sweet," you demonstrate understanding by beginning your next sentence with "Because it's sweet?" "How about you, which brand is your favorite?" You can also do this in the following ways: rephrasing what has been said with phrases like "What I'm hearing is..." or "It sounds like you're saying..."

Ask questions such as "What do you mean by..." or "Do you mean..."

Every now and then, repeat key words to the person.

That repetition of what the other person has said demonstrates that you are taking on board and listening to what they have to say, which means they will feel more open and connected with you.

- **Then React**

You can now respond because you've been actively listening to the other person and they've finished speaking. You don't want to fall into the trap of simply repeating what you wanted to say, but rather respond to what they're actually saying. You can accomplish this by: Addressing the main point of what they said once more for clarity

Pause for a few seconds to show that you're thinking about what they said. Convey your points as effectively as possible.

Don't be concerned about this last section because the rest of the book will be devoted to teaching you what to say in any situation, so we'll go over it all in greater detail.

The Synopsis

You'll notice a huge difference in how connected you are to other people in your conversations and how well you're being listened to if you use these techniques alone. When you listen to others and respect what they have to say, most people will do the same unconsciously back to you.

Tempers flare only when the other person does not feel heard or respected, and things spiral out of control. Remember that practice makes perfect, and simply incorporating these points into your next conversation will make a huge difference. Test it out for yourself!

To summarize, when listening to people, you should focus on the following: Understanding the two types of listening Practice listening to understand Avoid listening to respond Give someone your full attention Never interrupt someone Listen with your body, not just your ears Repeat back key points the other person said Respond to the point after everything else.

And so, we move on to the next chapter.

We'll be focusing on the core mechanics of actually speaking to someone and starting a conversation in one chapter, so if you want to skip ahead, no problem, but for clarity, the next chapter will explore some of the more advanced techniques you can use to listen more effectively actively.

Chapter 3

Improving Your Listening Skills

"No one is as deaf as a man who refuses to listen." — A proverb

A chapter that doesn't need an introduction because I just did it a minute ago, so let's get right into it.

Because everyone is different and we all have our own bad habits, some of these may apply to you and some may not, but I like to think of this section as a great reminder of how to listen as well as to help you set the overall intention of becoming a better listener.

Reduce Distractions

Larry D. Rosen Ph.D. conducted a study in 2012 on 300 middle school, high school, and university students to see how distracted they became depending on their environment.

Despite being surrounded by phones, computers, and televisions, the students were supposed to be studying.

The findings were startling, revealing that when surrounded by technology, students could only study for about three minutes at a time, with laptops and phones being the most distracting. It only takes three minutes. That's a really short attention span.

I understand that life is hectic and that things must be completed. When there aren't enough hours in the day, multitasking is sometimes the only viable option for getting things done. However, if you want to have meaningful conversations and connect with people, you'll need to sit down and talk to each other without the distractions we're usually surrounded by.

When someone is speaking to you, you can reduce distractions by: putting your phone down and locking it; turning off the TV; turning off your computer monitor; and not eating or drinking while talking with someone.

These tips will improve your conversations and relationships regardless of where you are or what you are doing, whether you are at home or at work.

Be Devoid of Judgments

It's critical to consider how your decisions affect your ability to listen. If you're set in your ways and feeling closed-minded or defensive about a subject, you may end up zoning out or preparing to tell them why they're wrong.

If you can step outside of that and open your mind, you might hear something or learn something new. You may even be able to sway your opinion or provide additional information to help you solidify your feelings. In any case, listening will help you grow as a person, so don't let the judgments stop you from doing so!

Focus on being more open-minded, noticing judgments when they arise, becoming more accepting of other people's ideas, and accepting people's flaws to become less judgmental.

Pose the Correct Questions

Active listening is all about understanding the other person, which is what communication is all about in general.

Whether you're sharing thoughts or ideas, attempting to solve a problem, or simply entertaining, you must be understanding, and others must understand you.

Sometimes people aren't the best communicators, and you'll need a little more information to understand them, which is fine.

However, because this is such an important consideration, we'll go over it in greater depth in the following chapter, so stay tuned!

The Synopsis

For the time being, these techniques and strategies should be sufficient to assist you in becoming the best listener possible. Some may seem obvious to you, while others may not have occurred to you, so pick and choose what you want to work on, and chances are you will see positive results even with your first interactions after reading this chapter, so good luck, and see it all in action for yourself.

Let's continue our exploration of the art of conversing with anyone.

Chapter 4

It's All About Questions

"At the end of the day, the questions we ask ourselves determine the kind of people we become."

-Leo Babauta's

We finished the previous chapter by discussing the importance of asking the right questions, and it's a subject that deserves a lot of attention. That's because, when it comes to talking to anyone about anything, having the ability to ask the right questions at the right time is the best strategy you can ever have on your side.

It is fairly self-explanatory. By asking questions, you can steer the conversation in whatever direction you want, gain clarity on what the other person is saying, and find common ground and similar interests. Everything revolves around questions!

Remember, you don't want to interrogate someone by bombarding them with questions. Instead, strike a balance between asking questions and talking, just as it's critical to get the topic of your questions correct. When you combine your newfound listening skills with your newfound ability to ask questions, you've got yourself a great conversation on your hands!

The Influence of Questions

You must be direct with your questions and use this powerful conversational tool to make the other person feel comfortable talking to you, to guide the conversation, and to make the other person feel understood.

Each of these components will be referred to as: Clarity, Direction and Understanding.

All of these things are necessary if you want to have a proper, meaningful conversation.

Assume you're having a conversation with a coworker. It's Monday morning, and everyone is getting ready for work.

"Hey! How are you doing? "How did your weekend go?"

"It was fine. Really, I just watched Netflix. "And how about you?"

"Yeah, it was fine. On Saturday, we had a barbeque, and on Sunday, we just puttered around the house."

Not the most enthralling conversation ever, but it's a fairly common one. You can now use questions in a variety of ways in this context.

If you want to be directed, you could ask, "What did you watch on Netflix?" Personally, I'm looking for something exciting. "I just finished Breaking Bad, and I have to say, it's really good."

You're now steering the conversation towards Netflix and TV shows, which is a perfectly acceptable small-talk topic, especially if action-packed shows are something you both enjoy. You've taken command of the conversation.

Other times, you'll want some clarification, and this is useful for ensuring that you understood the other person correctly. You also make the other person feel as if you are genuinely interested in what they have to say, making them feel more connected to you and more open to the topic at hand. Using the same example as before, you get the response: "I got a new dog this weekend."

What would your reaction be? Would you like to know what it's called? What is its age? The breed? If you don't know much about dog breeds, asking for the dog's breed isn't really a genuine question because once they answer, you'll be at a loss for what to say next.

Never just ask the question you believe is correct because you're going through the motions. Make a concerted effort to come up with better, more progressive questions. This is what it means to pose the appropriate questions.

Instead, how about something like, "Oh yeah? "How is he or she adjusting?"

Interesting. This isn't your typical question. It takes some thought. The person you're speaking with becomes more involved in the conversation.

"Actually, it's not too bad. He is, however, beginning to chew the edges of the sofa. I'm not sure if he's teething or not because he's so young."

What is your response? Another query? What would you choose? It's entirely up to you. Just keep in mind that you have three main options: Direction, Clarity, and Understanding.

If you want to be directed, you can say whatever you want, depending on which part of the conversation you want to enter. Let's say you're tired of talking about dogs and want to move on. You could say something like, "This could be a good excuse to get a new sofa." Alternatively, you could completely renovate. "Would you do it if you could?"

You're diverting the dog conversation to something a little more amusing or hypothetical. Let's say it's a little lighthearted. If you wanted clarification, for example, because you were aware of dogs' ability to bite through the corners of sofas, you could say something like, "Oh really? "Does the dog chew it all the time or only at certain times of the day?"

You're now looking for answers and delving deeper into the subject. If, on the other hand, you want the other person to feel understood, you can repeat back what they are saying.

"If it's a puppy, it could be an age thing." Have you done any research or spoken with a veterinarian?"

Of course, there are infinite ways to guide the conversation based on the questions you ask, but this should give you a good idea of how powerful questions are when it comes to communicating and a big part of talking to anyone.

Consider it this way. If you're asking questions and the other person is speaking, you don't even need to be speaking most of the time, which means there's little effort or chance for you to become anxious!

Using Questions to Begin Conversations

Of course, one of the most effective ways to use questions is to start conversations in the first place. However, you do not want to be monotonous. There's no denying that standard questions like "How are you?" and "Where are you from?" are tedious and overused. These are not the most effective ways to initiate a conversation.

There are unquestionably better options available.

So, let's take it one step at a time.

First and foremost, you must initiate the conversation. I'm assuming you're not just talking to a random stranger on the street, but rather to a colleague at work, a new client, as part of a networking event while on a date, or something similar.

However, if you do want to talk to a stranger on the street, always begin with a conversation about something in your immediate surroundings, such as asking for directions, a good place to eat, the time, or commenting on something that is going on around you.

For example, if a carnival is taking place, you could ask, "When was the last time you went to one of these?"

Let's pretend you're talking to someone you know in a familiar setting. It's time to start having some decent conversations. Here are some questions that can start a great conversation in a variety of situations.

Getting to Know Someone New (Networking, social event, etc.)

Tell me a little bit about yourself.

This is a great question because you let the other person take control and tell you what they want you to know, because no one will tell you anything they don't want you to know, allowing you to gain a true understanding of who this person is and what they're all about.

What was the highlight of your week?

This is one of my favorite questions because it shifts the tone of the conversation and allows the other person to reflect on what is important to them. They will experience positive emotions when they think about positive things. It's far superior to "How are you?"

Are you currently working on anything exciting?

Another opportunity for someone to be enthusiastic about talking to you, this question is ideal for when you want someone to be passionate about something.

Of course, they'll talk about the most important thing in their lives, which is another great way to get to know someone and learn about their priorities.

Have you visited this location before?

An open-ended question that can be used to determine someone's familiarity with a location or person. You'll get a good sense of how connected this person is if you're in a meeting or at an event, such as a business meeting, social event, birthday party (did you come last year?), and so on.

Other questions to ask when getting to know someone, particularly on a professional level, include:

- Where did you go to school?
- What did you enjoy most about school?
- How did you get into this industry?

- Do you believe your career path is similar to that of others?
- What is the most difficult challenge in your professional life?
- What do you enjoy most about your job?
- Is your day filled with a variety of activities?
- What is a typical workweek like for you?
- What are your future plans or aspirations?
- What is it like to work in your office?

Of course, once you've asked these questions, they'll naturally lead to other questions that will delve deeper into the topic you've chosen, depending on their responses.

Questions to Ask on a First Date

What do you like to do in your spare time?

- Do you prefer the morning or the evening?
- What would your ideal job be?
- Who is the most intriguing person you've ever met?
- What would your friends say about you?
- What song or artist never gets old to you?
- Which animal do you think is the cutest?
- Which animal do you think is the most unattractive?
- What city would you most like to live in?
- What is your proudest achievement?

- When was the last time you sang to yourself, and what song did you sing?
- What trends have you been unable to comprehend?
- Which "thing" reveals the most about a person?
- What was the most unusual turning point in your life?

Fun, Personal Small-Talk Questions to Ask Anyone, Anywhere

These are fun little questions you can ask anyone, whether you're talking to coworkers, friends, on a date, or just passing the time in a line somewhere.

There are a lot of fun questions you can ask people, and while they may sound a little strange, you'll usually find that people enjoy answering them because they can have so many interesting answers, especially if you're with a group of people, allowing you to compare and casually critique each other's answers.

Essentially, these are engaging conversation starters that anyone can participate in. Excellent for one-on-one or group conversations!

- What do you hope will never change in the world?
- What is your ideal vehicle?
- What's your go-to song when you're in a bad mood?

- What would you learn if you could learn any skill?
- What subject do you wish you knew more about?
- How has your life changed in the last year?
- What is the farthest you've traveled from home?
- Where would you go if you could visit any fictional location?

How to Ask the Right Questions

Locate the Line

Just a quick note, more of a disclaimer than anything else: don't jump right in and start asking really personal or sensitive questions, such as race, sex, politics, religion, and so on. These can be contentious issues, and while it would be ideal to live in a world where we could all discuss things openly and without judgment, we're not quite there yet.

Instead, save these discussions for when the time and place are right, or when you're with people you trust and are comfortable enough with to have them.

Consider the Social Hierarchy.

Personally, I think it's a shame that we can't just be ourselves in front of everyone (and I know, a lot of what I've already said is about being yourself), but for many other people, you won't be able to connect with them unless you speak to them in a way they'll understand.

If you're talking to a peer or colleague, for example, you'll use different language and come across differently than if you're talking to your boss. Similarly, you would address the president or the Queen of England in a different manner.

When speaking with others, try to adjust your tone of voice and the questions you ask so that they are most effective for the listener.

If you're speaking to a client who is quite a fancy person, speaking in a genuinely "fancy" manner will make them connect with you far more than filling your sentences with slang.

"Ah, yes, we're very excited about the project." "How do you feel about it so far?"

"Yeah, the project is coming along nicely. "Are you eager to get started?"

The question is the same in both cases; it's just how the question is phrased that differs.

Keep Your Inquiries Open-Ended

Finally, because you're inviting someone to give you a comprehensive answer, try to keep your questions as open-ended as possible.

"How are you doing?"

"Good."

That is not a good conversation to be having.

"Can you tell me about the highlight of your week?"

"That's an excellent question. Let me think about it. Probably getting a free panini at my favorite cafe because they know me and are nice."

"Wow, that's awesome that they did that. "Have you been going there for a long time?"

Much more intriguing. While we're on the subject, you can make questions more open-ended by including words like what, who, and how. You can also say, "Tell me more," which allows someone to elaborate on what they're saying.

With that, you should have a better understanding of how important it is to ask questions in your conversations, as well as the benefits you can gain from doing so.

The Synopsis

To summarize this chapter, remember to:

- Ask lots of questions to get to know someone.
- Keep the questions open-ended by using words like what and how.
- Use questions to direct the conversation, clarify points, or gain a better understanding.
- Depending on the situation, keep a list of go-to questions handy.
- Avoid getting too personal or delving into sensitive topics.

Armed with this new knowledge, I'm going to take you down a different rabbit hole, which is being able to talk to someone in the first place, regardless of the situation.

Chapter 5

How to Have a Conversation with Anyone

"A good conversation can excite you more than alcohol; it can refresh you more than the theater or a concert." It can provide you with entertainment and pleasure; it can help you get ahead, solve problems, and inspire others' imaginations. It has the potential to broaden your knowledge and education. It has the power to clear up misunderstandings and bring you closer to those you care about."

— Dorothy S. Sarnoff

This next chapter is essentially the book's climax.

Within the next few pages, I'll share and explore a literal step-by-step method for having a conversation with anyone about anything. In the following chapters, we'll talk more about what you can talk about and how to carry these conversations to make them even better, but for now, we'll cover the absolute basics, laying the groundwork for your future conversations.

Ready? Let's get started.

Step One - Make a Good First Impression

First impressions are always important, so how do you want others to perceive yours?

After all, even if it may not appear so at times, you have complete control over it.

As a side note, this section could also cover topics like dressing well, dressing for the occasion, making sure your personal hygiene is up to par, and so on, because these are all critical points to remember if you want to connect with someone and make a good first impression.

Keeping with the interpersonal conversational skills theme, whenever you meet someone new, you'll want to make a good first impression so that they can connect with you. After all, while we're taught not to judge a book by its cover, let's face it: we all do it all the time. When you go on a first date or meet a new client, you judge that person to see if they're someone you want to work with or spend more time with.

Furthermore, while you are making your first impression on them, they are also making one on you. So, what do they have to say? There's a lot to consider, but let's look at both sides of the first impressions coin.

Examining the Situation

Remember when your teacher called in sick and you had a substitute teacher to cover for them in school?

I remember having one in my French class, and for the first few lessons, everyone was polite and kept quiet. While this was completely unintentional, it's clear in retrospect that we were trying to figure out whether the teacher was extremely strict or a bit of a pushover. As we became more at ease and pushed the boundaries, we began to misbehave more and more, as most children do.

The class gradually descended into chaos as soon as it became clear that the teacher was trying to be a "cool" teacher and wasn't going to crack a whip in our direction for the slightest problem.

This logic applies to your own conversations and interactions as well.

When you enter a new interaction, begin by reading the other person and determining what type of person they are. Test the waters and see what kind of response you get. Some questions to ask and things to pay attention to include:

- What kind of tone of voice do they use?
- What are their clothes like?
- Are they occupied?
- Are they working or relaxing?
- Do they appear stressed?
- Are they grinning?
- How strong is their handshake?
- Are they on time to meet you?
- What does their body language say to you?
- How courteous are they?
- What kind of manners do they have?
- What do your instincts tell you about them?

Some people are much easier to read than others, and you may immediately recognize the type of person you're speaking with, especially if they're very forthcoming. Alternatively, you may need to gauge a little and get the conversation going to truly get a sense of who this person is and, as a result, how you'll effectively communicate with them.

For example, if someone is withdrawn, is it because they are shy or because they are trying to hide something?

Your current situation will provide a lot of context. The trick here is to ignore what the person is saying and instead read their body language and all of the other factors we've discussed. Body language, on the other hand, is extremely important.

According to research, body language accounts for approximately 55% of all communication, and tone of voice accounts for 30%, so be aware of it!

Some tips to keep in mind when reading body language are as follows:

- Posture is important. Is someone's head up and confident, or is he or she unsure and looking down, avoiding eye contact?
- Appearance. What are they dressed in? Casual? Smart? Relaxed? Doesn't give a damn?
- Crossed arms and legs are often used to express defensive feelings.
- Hands in pockets (or hidden hands) indicate that the person is concealing something
- Lip biting or nail picking can be a sign of stress.

By observing these characteristics, you should be able to read the other person you're speaking with fairly well, and you can then use this information to respond appropriately.

Remember that people will respond to you based on how they perceive you to be speaking to them, so adjust your communication style for the best results. When you begin to get to know someone and develop a deeper relationship with them, you can begin to reveal more of yourself.

Speaking to someone who appears shy, stressed, or sad is an example of an initial conversation. If you notice these signs, you should approach them nicer, more compassionate than you would normally speak to someone.

Even if you're having trouble reading someone, keep this in mind: When it comes to picking up on cues, your gut instinct is usually correct, so trust it.

According to research, people who are more tuned into sensing their body sensations in high-pressure situations (in the study's case, people who worked on high-stress London trading floors) make better, more successful decisions than those who are out of sync with their gut instinct.

In other words, if you have a feeling and your body makes you feel a certain way, your body is trying to tell you something, so listen to it!

Creating a Room

Along with the preceding point, it's critical to apply what you've learned to take control of your own first impressions and adjust how others perceive you. If you walk into a room crashing around and stumbling, then hide in the corner, you make a very different impression than someone who walks in and sits down gracefully and confidently.

- You have complete control over this!
- Some quick points to consider are:
- How you dress
- Your tone of voice when speaking; and what your body language says about you.
- The strength of your handshake
- Are you looking the other person in the eyes?
- Are you staring too long?
- Are you paying full attention to someone, or are you distracted?

Be aware of how you present yourself to others, and you will receive a reaction based on what you do. This gives you complete control of a situation when speaking with anyone, making you feel far more confident in your ability to communicate.

Another excellent example can be found in Patrick King's Better Small Talk. In his book, he discusses children and how they lack the social filters that many of us develop as we get older.

We have insecurities, anxieties, and characteristics that children do not yet have. This is why, when we talk to children, we speak to them in a specific manner based on how they speak to us.

In most cases, younger children will simply act naturally. This is why children will happily cry in public or behave the same way in front of elderly relatives as they do in front of younger family members. Kids are their true selves, often to amusing or embarrassing ends.

However, children's confidence in simply being themselves means that they are confidently writing the room around them, in which adults will follow suit and respond in a certain way.

This is why it's so easy to talk to children: they can speak with such confidence, without censorship, and with such openness.

Step 2: Make Your First Move

There's no denying that many of us place so much emphasis on "breaking the ice" and making the first move, almost certainly to the point where we're so afraid to speak first that we don't speak at all. We've arrived at this point because we've had to retrain ourselves to be more confident over time. There's a huge fear that we'll be rejected by the other person, judged, or hurt in some way, even if we're just asking a stranger for directions on the street.

Allow that to sink in and consider how true it is for many people!

On the other hand, making the first move is critical if you want success in your conversation and not just success in making it happen in the first place. According to one study, making the first move results in great success in many areas of your life. Making the first offer in business gives you more control and increases your chances of getting a better deal. Making the first move in dating increases your chances of getting what you want.

But how do you gain the courage to do it?

The reality is that breaking the ice and making the first move isn't all that difficult. All you have to do is "cut the fluff" and get to the point. I could simply say, "Be confident," "Don't put too much pressure on yourself and the end result," and "Be in the moment," but I'm guessing that doesn't really help, so let's break it down.

Consider dating (I like using this example a lot because we tend to put so much pressure on ourselves in these situations, most of the time unnecessarily).

When trying to ask someone out, there's a whole taboo subject that you need to have "game." You have to be slick and have "tactics" to make it work, but this isn't real life, and it won't get you anywhere.

For some reason, we've forgotten that simply approaching someone and being our genuine, authentic selves is by far the best way to get someone's attention and build a much stronger connection in the long run. Of course, this applies to any situation, not just dating.

That doesn't help you make the first move, though. You may feel as if you are bothering someone by speaking to them, holding them up, or interrupting them. You may be hesitant to approach a stranger for fear of upsetting them or annoying them. This is a case of social anxiety in full swing.

What is the next step?

Approach someone indirectly for something, for some reason, and keep this reason in mind at all times, but don't make it a long-term reason. Don't think to yourself, "Wow, I want to talk to this person because I want to date and marry them, and so on."

Thinking this way indicates that you are putting far too much pressure on yourself because rejection will hurt. There's too much emphasis on the outcome, and it'll cause you to buckle when the conversations become too intense.

Begin small. Consider, "Hey, this person seems nice." I'll ask if they'd like to FaceTime or go out to dinner. Asking someone to dinner is a much smaller commitment than thinking long term, and you don't even need the pressure of such an event if it's too much.

Make a reason to talk to someone, even if you don't have one. Again, this is an excellent practice because it allows you to try something new, boost your confidence, and improve your communication skills. Most interactions will not be the most important ones you'll ever have, so relax and enjoy them!

Some things you can say or ask are:

- Do you have the time?
- Where can I find the nearest bank?
- Is the food good in this restaurant?
- What time does the show begin?
- Have you seen this film before?
- I enjoy the music here.
- Do you know anyone around here?

These are all small statements you can make to break the ice, allowing you to engage in small talk and conversation, and eventually a deeper connection if you want to continue speaking with them.

Step Three - Locate the Link

You're now conversing with someone you approached properly, the ice has broken, and the conversation is beginning to pick up and find its own pace. What should you do now?

The best way to find a connection is to look for similarities between yourself and the other person. This includes finding common ground on things you're interested in, whether it's a hobby, passion, or music taste, or even simply commenting on and sharing opinions on what's going on in your immediate environment or situation. A good example of the latter is commenting on the music at a concert.

This is where your listening skills come into play, because you're focusing on what someone is saying (as well as what their body language is saying) and then picking out the bits that seem most connected to them, then running with it. Allow me to give you an example.

Assume you're at a concert and making small talk with someone at the bar. Your initial impression is that they aren't having a good time. They just stare into their drink, not paying attention to the music, and appear to be mentally elsewhere.

Everything about them suggests they're going through a difficult time, so you choose to be compassionate and inquire if everything is okay, perhaps saying something like, "Is the music too loud for you?" This is lighthearted and not too personal, but it also implies that you recognize that something isn't right and are willing to talk to them about it.

You can then figure out what's wrong and how to deal with the situation based on their response, and you could be on your way to making a close friend.

In any given situation, depending on the context, you can find common ground by asking questions such as:

- Where did you go to school?
- What is your place of employment?
- What sports team do you root for?
- What kind of music do you like?
- What is your favorite food?
- Where do you prefer to eat?
- What kinds of movies do you like to watch?

It's also critical to make your feelings known about what you agree on. It's all well and good to think ("Hey, me too!"), but you won't connect with the other person unless you tell them you're on the same page. This is a great way to establish rapport and make someone want to connect with you, which brings us nicely to the next point.

The Art of Mirroring

Mirroring is an essential part of any conversation because it makes you more relatable to the person with whom you're conversing. Mirroring is a practice in which you consciously copy (but not too obviously) the tone of voice, posture, body language, speed of speech, and overall physical appearance of the person to whom you're speaking, which dramatically improves how connected people feel to you.

You can also mirror based on the language and visual style of the person speaking to you, such as the amount of slang they use, but physical mirroring is sufficient for most conversations.

A study (Anderson, 1998) also discovered that when mirroring occurs, people feel more positive toward strangers.

Using the bar as an example, if someone is slouching at the bar and you pull up next to them and do the same, you are mirroring. If they speak slowly and without enthusiasm, mirroring this will help them absorb what you're saying more effectively because you've already established common ground through physical acts.

Some things to keep in mind when mirroring someone are:

Mimicking voice speed and tone Mimicking gesture volume Mimicking body language, such as posture and leaning. The inflection on certain words Slang usage. The energy and excitement for a topic.

You know when you meet someone and discover that you both love the same band, movie franchise, or sports team, and you look at each other like, "Oh my god, you love them too?" That's incredible!" and your energy levels skyrocket, as if you're both building momentum with each other? That's the power of mirroring in action.

Step Four - Dealing with Potential Obstacles

If you follow the three steps above, you'll be able to talk to anyone about anything, so we'll end the book there. Thank you for your time. Have a wonderful day.

Of course, I'm joking. In an ideal situation, you will follow these points, and people will respond positively to you, allowing the conversations to flow naturally from here on out. However, not everyone is relatable in this way, and conversing with some people can be as boring as conversing with a brick wall.

This can happen for a variety of reasons, including the person having a bad day, being surprised that you are talking to them in the first place, being stressed out, being shy and anxious, or simply not being in the mood to talk.

When you're talking to people like this, and the conversation feels like it's squeezing by with friction, it can be difficult to know what to say next. Do you try to persuade the conversation to continue, or do you cut and run?

To begin, keep in mind that you can always leave a conversation if you don't want to continue. Simply say something like, "Oh, I've got to dash to make the train/get some food/meet someone else," and you can leave.

However, there may be times when you need to speak with someone, such as when conversing with someone at work, attempting to complete a task, interviewing someone, networking, or attempting to obtain information from them. Don't worry; it's not as bad as it sounds. Assume you're planning a surprise party for someone and need to know their schedule without telling them what's going on.

How can you move the discussion forward?

Elicitation, a communication technique developed by the FBI for interrogation purposes, is perhaps the most commonly used technique here. I'm not suggesting that you go out and question people for information—far from it. Teachers use this technique in the classroom all the time, perhaps without realizing where it came from.

Elicitation is the process of persuading people to share information that they are holding onto by using statements that coerce the person into speaking even if they do not want to.

Recognizing and complimenting someone is an example of this.

Human beings, while complex, are actually quite simple in terms of how we function. We are social creatures who are hardwired to seek praise and recognition from others because it shows that we have been accepted into a larger group, which was necessary for our survival in tribes and larger groups back in the day.

Giving someone a compliment on how they look or how they act can be a great way to get them to talk. You could say something like, "I really like your coat." It suits you. Damn, I love how hardworking you are. Your attention to detail is incredible, and you have a great way of expressing yourself.

Another way to engage in elicitation is to complain, and as you're probably aware, humans love to mutually dislike someone, whether it's an opposing sports team, the grey weather, or simply a mutually shared situation, such as having to stay late after work to finish a project.

People enjoy whining. According to studies, the average person complains 15-30 times per day, and ActofLibraries.com ranks "starting a conversation" as the top reason for complaining in the first place.

A quick complaint into something can be a very powerful way to open people up and get them speaking, especially if they're looking to vent about a problem they're having.

With all of this in mind, the next time you watch a crime thriller or detective series with a police interview, you might notice these tactics in full effect. I recently sat down to watch Breaking Bad again and saw the episode where Brock is poisoned and Jesse has to go into the police station to explain why he believes Brock was poisoned by a super-rare substance (mild spoiler alert).

The detectives say things like, "We don't need to involve the lawyers." It's all pen-pushing and a lot of hassle, and we understand how stressful these situations can be. Simply unwind. We're simply chatting.

You're a wise man, Jesse, as well as a kind and caring individual. We know you only want to do the right thing.

Even when someone is being interrogated for an alleged crime, detectives use compliments to encourage them to talk, even if they don't want to.

This brings us to the end of this chapter. To summarize, when it comes to starting a conversation, you should: read the other person, aim to create the first impression you want to give, break the ice with a question, have a goal in mind for the conversation, find similar interests, find the connection you share, mirror the person you're speaking to and practice talking to unresponsive people.

Chapter 6

Mastering the Art of Small Talk

"The smallest talk we do is the biggest talk we do." Susan RoAne

The main issue my friend Kyle encountered while attending his sister's wedding was not being able to start a conversation in the first place, and I know from personal experience that this is one of the most difficult aspects of meeting and getting to know new people.

Before I met my current partner, I spent a lot of time on dating apps like Tinder and Bumble, and I always struggled with what to say after the initial "hey" (which was usually followed by a cringey waving emoji, but I won't get into that). But, then, what are you supposed to say in order to be interesting, charismatic, and genuinely interesting to others?

Other times in my life, such as lining up at the gym to get into a spinning class, I'm surrounded by strangers, and you make the generic small talk about the weather and the problems and politics of the gym, poor management, and so on, but where do you go from there? You're not going to be best friends with someone who talks like that.

That's what I'm going to devote this chapter to: mastering small talk.

Every single relationship you've ever had (except perhaps with your parents or siblings) would have begun with some form of small talk. A litmus test to see if the person is someone you connect with or not, if you want to be friends with them or not, if you want to work with them or not, and so on.

Mastering this art, like listening, will take some practice, but with the knowledge we'll cover in this chapter, you'll be set for success. So, let's get started.

The Fundamentals of Small Talk

To begin, it's worth noting that, like listening, the art of small talk appears to have an infinite depth, and it's a lifelong skill that you can always work on improving. With over nine billion people on the planet, there will always be a new way to communicate with someone and a new way to learn.

That being said, the art of small talk can be reduced to four core foundations upon which everything else is built. Fortunately, the first three steps are things you already know: ask questions (especially open-ended ones), listen actively, and minimize distractions.

So, what is the fourth, enigmatic foundation? Any ideas?

It is, in fact, displaying zeal. Adding vigor to your conversations. Demonstrating your enthusiasm. Infuse vibrancy into your interactions. As long as you are enthusiastic, you can talk about anything and it will be engaging.

The Influence of Enthusiasm

Small talk isn't the most interesting thing in the world, but that's just the generic small talk we've all become so painfully accustomed to. Showing energy and enthusiasm for connection, no matter what you're talking about, can be such a powerful gateway into having a deeper relationship, and it helps the person you're speaking with open up and be themselves, thus nurturing a meaningful relationship even further.

Even if you just act enthusiastic about even the most mundane conversations, you'll notice a change in how you interact with others. Try it out in your head right now. Consider a typical conversation with someone in your life, and then imagine that same conversation with three times the zeal, and consider how they would react. I'm not saying you have to be like this all of the time, or that you have to give it ten times the effort when talking about traffic. You choose the times and locations where you want to go all in.

It all comes down to your attitude and intentions when it comes to bringing this level of energy to your conversations. If you go into any conversation, professional or personal, friends or family, lovers or children, with the mindset that you want to know more about this person, or you just want to have fun or learn something new, you'll suddenly start viewing human interaction in a completely different way, and your life will change as a result.

You'll quickly realize that there are an infinite number of people to meet, infinite points of view and perspectives to learn from, and amusing stories and experiences to share, and aren't these the values you were looking for when you picked up this book in the first place?

So, how do you go about it?

It can be difficult to bring enthusiasm to a conversation, especially if you aren't naturally energetic, and going above and beyond how you would normally be may make you feel fake or as if you're not truly being yourself, but this isn't a path you want to take. You want to be genuine in your energy levels.

Fortunately, there are numerous ways to accomplish this.

Act More Activated

Even minor changes in your conversational style can make a significant difference. You can speak a little louder (I'm not saying shout), and you can change your tone of voice to make it more varied. You can also emphasize specific words and change your inflection to make what you're saying more interesting to hear.

Consider the following two sentences:

Over the weekend, I got a new cat.

Oh my goodness, I got a NEW cat over the weekend, and she's ADORABLE!

The emphasis is on the big words, and you can see how just slightly changing what you're saying can give your words so much more power.

Of course, you can amplify your body language to complement what you're saying. For example, rather than saying, "Well, you have two options. "A or B?" You can highlight the options by indicating right for A and left for B with your hands. You're not really pointing at anything, but you're emphasizing the fact that there is a decision to be made and two options to consider.

In general, this type of action makes the conversation appear more interactive.

- Highlight Your Emotions

You don't have to agree with everything anyone says to you in order for them to like you. In fact, it's better if you surround yourself with people who hold opposing viewpoints because it helps you get out of your own head.

There will be things you disagree with, as well as statements that resonate with you, but whatever you feel, emphasize that this is how you feel. This is one of the most effective ways to inject energy into a conversation because it allows you to simply be yourself.

For example, if someone says something that you agree with or that you couldn't have said better yourself, tell that person how you feel. Consider the following statements:

Yes! I wholeheartedly concur. You phrased it far better than I could!

I'm glad you mentioned it. I share your sentiments!

What's that? You're interested in that as well?

I understand what you're saying, but I'm the polar opposite. I adore XYZ.

I completely disagree with you. I truly believe...

Consider how much energy statements like these can bring to a conversation, as well as how validating they will feel for the other person.

Be honest and express your feelings. When you are open and honest, the conversation becomes less placid and passive and more direct and assertive.

- Utilize Natural Energy

Just a quick note here. I'm not here to tell you how to live a healthy life, but it's common knowledge that if you take care of your body, you naturally have a ton of untapped energy that will naturally rise up in how you live your life.

This includes regular exercise, a healthy diet, plenty of water, and getting enough sleep each night, among other things. You will naturally have more energy if you take care of yourself. This may all seem obvious, but I know for a fact that I used to not take care of myself properly, and taking control of that brought about a lot of positive changes. Surround Yourself with Like-Minded People

- Granted, you won't be surrounded by positive, happy people every waking moment of your life, and that wouldn't be healthy.

Sounds like there's some strange cult going on in that world. However, if you want to adopt these personality traits, you must have some stable positive people in your life with whom you spend regular time.

Negativity is physically and mentally draining, and you will not feel energetic or on the ball if you are depressed and drained. It just won't happen unless you're extremely committed to faking how you feel.

Spend time with people who give you energy, make you feel good, and don't consistently bring toxicity and negativity into your life.

Finding Interesting Small-Talk Topics

So you've been following the advice above, and you're starting to inject your own energy into your conversations.

It makes no difference where you are or who you are speaking with—you are appealing to listen to. You're also listening to the other person and asking questions, and everything appears to be going well. I'm sure you can see how everything we've already discussed is coming together to make your conversations unlike any other conversations you've ever had.

Remember how I said at the outset that being charismatic and confident is something that can be learned? Consider everything you've learned thus far and how applying this knowledge will change your relationships and interactions. Perhaps you've already tried it and are beginning to see the results? Fortunately, there's more to learn.

What actual topics you can talk about is a question we've been asked several times. While there are practically infinite topics to discuss, it can be difficult to remember the best ones, and while one person may be very interested in one topic, another person may have no interest at all, leaving you with no ideas on how to proceed. This section is here to assist you.

To get started, here are some great topics to keep in your back pocket that you can bring up in any conversation.

Talking about your current location (immediate environment) food, restaurants, and cooking, travel, vacations, holidays, dream destinations, sports, hobbies and interests, art favorite local places

When you enter a conversation with someone, if you listen carefully (which is why we covered this skill in the first chapters), you can pick up clues that will help you determine which topics to engage in. Here's an example of a conversation between two people while they wait quietly at a bus stop on a grey rainy day.

A: Hello. Are you all right? You have a gloomy expression on your face.

B: No, I'm fine. I've never been a fan of either waiting or rain.

Notice how they begin to discuss the weather? It's a typical small talk conversation about the immediate surroundings, which makes it easy to discuss, but what's interesting is that person B used it as an excuse for not feeling well right now. Listening to one sentence reveals all of this.

A: Oh, you're a sun worshipper?

B: Certainly. Every single day of the week.

A: Where would you go if you could travel anywhere in the world on a bus?

A lovely transition from traditional small talk to a more interesting topic of conversation that is open-ended enough for them to respond however they see fit. If they respond creatively, you know the person is ready to talk. If they're blunt and respond with something like, "Hm, I don't know," you can bet they're not in the mood.

B: Most likely in the south of France. It's fantastic down there. The sun shines brightly on the beach.

A: Oh, yes. Have you been there before? I'd like to visit there myself.

And so forth.

People will give you topics to talk about in everything they say, more than you probably realize, because they are constantly thinking about themselves and how they perceive the world. Person B in this example enjoys traveling abroad and spending time in the sun, as evidenced by the first thing they say.

Notice how person A ends with "I'd love to go there myself," bringing that energy and passion into the conversation and inviting person B to open up more and start sharing their energy for something they love—in this case, warm countries. They don't appear to be very engaged in the conversation at first, but after a few sentences, they can start to be themselves. The conversation settles into a rhythm.

You'll Have to Carry the Conversation... Initially

You may feel that this type of conversation is very one-sided, with you doing all the talking and the other person not really asking you questions, but that is unfortunately the way things are these days for many people. That is not to say that everyone is like this, but there are several reasons for it.

People either love talking about themselves or, especially if they're talking with a stranger, won't think to ask them about their lives or are too afraid to ask because they feel intrusive. Others may not be accustomed to conversing with others in such an open manner, so it may take some time for them to open up and come out of their shells.

There are numerous reasons why we have arrived at this point. According to studies and research, we're drifting apart from one another, or we're so reliant on social media that we're losing our social communication skills. Many studies, such as the 2018 study on "Social Media Use and Perceived Social Isolation Among Young Adults in the United States," show that social media use is a major contributor to ever-increasing feelings of isolation and loneliness, implying that we're disconnecting from one another like never before.

Everyone is different, and whatever the reason for someone being too withdrawn to talk to you and step out of their own shell is, you have the tools to help the people you speak with come out the other side and realize we don't have to be so closed off with each other.

Meaningful relationships take time to develop.

Going back to my line in the gym for a spinning class, there are plenty of topics to discuss with those around me. I could discuss the class's quality, the music selection, how easy it was to park outside this evening, gym announcements, and so on.

These may not appear to be particularly interesting topics at first glance, but that does not make them any less important. Remember, you never know what you'll learn or what topics of conversation will arise as a result of the typical small-talk topics, so try not to be judgmental.

Furthermore, making small talk about simple topics first is critical for opening the door to deeper conversations later on. If you're talking to someone, you need to establish a connection with them before moving on to deeper, more meaningful topics.

Trust and respect are essential components of any relationship, and they take time to develop.

My mother and father tried pottery classes when they first retired, which is a really beautiful example of this point.

When we caught up, they'd tell me about the dull conversations they'd had at first, and how these classes weren't for them. It was all small talk with no substance, gossip, and the like, none of which piqued my parents' interest. I told them to be patient and to give it some time. It was only because they were new and the relationships were forming that it was like this.

They learned that one of the other attendees, Maisie, was battling cancer, so on a Sunday afternoon walk, they took flowers and chocolates to her house as a surprise and had an afternoon of tea. Their friendship flourished, and once Maisie had recovered from her therapy, my parents, Maisie, her husband, and a few other students from the pottery class even went on vacation together.

On those first few sessions, all of these opportunities began with small talk in a pottery class. Every relationship must begin somewhere.

This is why it's a good idea to have a few key go-to small-talk topics on hand that you can use at any time. I know we've already covered a lot of topics you can discuss, but for the sake of completeness, here are a few more:

It's simple. It's in the middle. It is something that everyone can discuss. It's a great place to start. This is a great topic to practice and use to improve your skills if you're just starting out on your journey to becoming more confident with your small talk.

I'm curious who ordered this lovely weather.

Today feels like monsoon season.

I enjoy days with this kind of fog. It's unsettling.

Another fan favorite is entertainment. People are bound to be interested in something during their leisure time, whether it's books, movies, TV shows, cinema, sports, restaurants, or anything else. Get involved and find out what other people like.

Are you reading any good books right now? I'm looking for some good recommendations.

Do you like to listen to podcasts? I'm attempting to engage them.

Do you have any entertaining apps on your phone?

Which team do you cheer for?

Have you recently gone to the movies? I haven't been in a long time!

Are you currently watching the tennis championship?

Private Life

You don't want to get too personal with people you've just met (this can be perceived as too forward or even intrusive), but a few personal questions that help you get to know someone better are acceptable.

Where does your ancestors come from?

Have you ever looked into your family history?

How long have you been with your partner?

Have you got any brothers and sisters? (Pets is another good question.) I'm sure you get the idea. Other great topics to discuss include: hobbies, travel, food interests, celebrity gossip, and information about your hometown.

Work-life balance and career advancement

If you're stuck for ideas, you can always talk about what's going on right now in the location you're in. Listen carefully to find topics that both you and the other person are interested in. If one of you isn't interested in sports at all, it's not a good place to go (unless you're talking about how uneducated you are in sports, which can be quite amusing if communicated correctly).

Continue to ask questions and allow the topics of conversation to emerge naturally.

Topics to Avoid in Small Talk

I've talked a lot about small-talk topics you can get into, but very little about topics you should probably avoid talking about at all costs, which is what this section is all about. It's very easy to get caught up in and stuck talking about these topics, and while they may be fine for some people, I would avoid them in general.

Quick note: This isn't to say you can't ever discuss these topics with other people in your life, but they're usually reserved for conversations with people you can trust and know you can speak openly with.

Finances, I mean, imagine someone approaching you and asking you how much money you make. Because it's a sensitive subject, you're unlikely to be eager to share. Furthermore, how much we earn is usually only asked as a way to judge someone based on who they are, which no one wants. At all costs, avoid (no pun intended).

Religion

It's always a contentious subject. You never know what other people believe, so you should save this topic for when you know someone and have enough respect for each other to listen to each other and actually talk about how you feel on the subject, rather than passing judgment on someone you barely know.

Politics

As with religion, the topic of politics has the potential to become extremely emotionally charged and out of hand, especially when you are unaware of the other person's point of view. There may be times and places when it's appropriate, but generally, avoid this topic until you've gotten to know someone well.

The end of life

This topic should probably be on this list without needing to be mentioned, but if you want to have a positive conversation with someone you want to get to know, you should probably avoid heavy topics like death and loss. These can be emotionally charged and upsetting, which are not emotions you want to be associated with in your first meetings.

Sexing

Sex is a private matter. Making jokes, dropping innuendos, and openly discussing sex with strangers has the potential to make people feel extremely uncomfortable, and they will remember you negatively. Sure, there may be times when it's appropriate to discuss it, such as when you're flirting, but you'll want to choose your moments wisely.

Health and happiness

Have you ever been talking to someone and accidentally mentioned that you're not feeling well, and they immediately jump in with all these quick fixes and remedies? It's the most vexing thing, especially when the other person has no idea about the specifics of your condition or its complexities (and isn't usually a trained healthcare professional). Don't let yourself become that person.

Personal life slander

Talk about celebrity gossip because these are people who have made their lives public, but sharing gossip about people in your life is not a good idea. While people may be engaged and interested in what you're saying, this topic paints you in a negative light, and people will avoid you consciously if you end up sharing personal information about them.

Inappropriate jokes

Sure, you can tell your most sexist, racist, and offensive jokes when you're with people you care about, whether they're friends or family. I'm not advocating hatred, but I recognize that comedy is comedy, regardless of its form. However, sharing these with people you don't know is extremely risky and could land you in serious trouble. Imaginesharing one on your first day at a new job and pushing everyone away. It's a bad situation.

Physical Appearance

It's a fairly common topic to avoid. Because you don't know how sensitive someone is, it's best not to ask how old they are or make comments about their physical appearance. A common example is asking someone how far along they are in their pregnancy when they aren't even pregnant. Consider yourself in that situation.

Ex-partners or friendships

When you're on a first date with someone, it's pretty obvious that you don't want to start talking about your ex. It's a bitter place to take the conversation, and it's likely to turn negative, which is not something you want to be associated with when people are spending time with you. Avoid!

Are there any restricted conversation topics?

Let's say you start talking about your hobbies, such as swimming, but the other person has no interest in swimming and hasn't swum in years. Why do you insist on talking about swimming? It's as if you're trying to bore and push the other person away. If someone does not appear to be interested in the topic of conversation, change it up.

Putting the Conversation to Rest

In many ways, how you end a conversation is as important as how you begin it. While you've already made your first impression, how you end an interaction will determine how people treat you the next time you see them.

This is why it's a good idea to practice and rehearse some key exit lines that you can always fall back on to leave a good impression. Here are a few suggestions to get you started.

It's been a pleasure meeting you. Do you have a phone number or a social media account?

I'm looking forward to hearing how your project/meeting/event goes. When will we meet again?

This has been fantastic. I'll go get something to eat. Will you be around?

Wow. It is true that you can learn something new every day. Thank you very much. I have to leave now, but would it be okay to swap details and continue this later?

You'll need to adjust what you say, the words you use, and the way you say it depending on the situation, just as we've done with every other aspect of conversation. You'll speak differently to a professional client than you would to someone you're asking out on a date, for example, but you can be creative.

The best idea, however, is to think about how you can positively sign off on a conversation, make your exit, and leave the situation so that the person you were speaking with remembers you and this experience positively.

Developing the Art of Small Talk

All of the methods and topics we've covered in this chapter are excellent for improving your small-talk skills, but as I've said before, simply reading about them won't make you any better. Only through practice will you improve.

I like the metaphor, so I'll repeat it (probably for the last time, I promise...maybe).

You must spend time in the pool if you want to improve your swimming abilities.

If you're wondering how to "get in the pool" when it comes to small talk, this section has you covered as we look at some of the ways you can incorporate small talk into your daily life and thus become better at it.

Keep an eye out for opportunities.

By speaking with a variety of people about a variety of topics, you'll begin to develop your own opening and closing statements, as well as a real sense of how you can traverse various topics of conversation and what subjects you can discuss passionately.

However, all of these social aspects come with experience, so get some!

Keep an eye out for opportunities to practice small talk no matter what you're doing or where you are in your life.

Speak with the store's cashier. The person in line behind you.The man behind the bar.Following the lesson, the class teacher. I can't emphasize enough how much practice will help you. Of course, not everyone will be interested in talking for various reasons, but that's fine. Just keep going and you'll get better. Experiment with things that are out of your comfort zone!

Assume you're Friends

This was perhaps the most significant game-changer in my personal small-talk improvement journey, as it opened so many doors.

For many years, I worked in sales and found it difficult to communicate with new clients and project managers. I could present my projects and proposals because I had a plan, but I was useless when it came to anything else.

However, once I changed my mindset to believe that anyone I was speaking with was already a friend, someone I knew, or someone I could trust and was close to, I unconsciously began treating them as friends, which meant I was more open, confident, and charismatic.

It's a quick mental shift—a trick, if you will—that can help you relax and become more comfortable in your own skin.

Be Kind to Yourself.

You will make mistakes on your journey to self-improvement. While these can be embarrassing, especially when it comes to talking with new people with whom you're attempting to build a positive relationship, they're all part of the journey and something you'll look back on in years to come and laugh at while marveling at how far you've come.

Making mistakes isn't a big deal, and if you try to protect yourself in life so that you never make mistakes, you'll never get anywhere or learn the lessons that will change your life.

Establish Goals

While small talk is not a military operation, despite how it may appear at times, it can really help you have direction with what you say if you set goals and targets for your conversations. Consider Kyle's attendance at his sister's wedding. Is he just having a good time? Become acquainted with others? Have a good laugh? Have you met someone?

Having a clear objective allows you to determine how much energy you're bringing to the table, what topics you want to cover, and who you're going to spend your time speaking to.

The Synopsis

That's it! Wasn't that a good start? When it comes to mastering small talk, the core points you'll want to focus on practicing are: being energetic and enthusiastic, being genuinely yourself regarding your interests, becoming confident with a variety of small-talk topics, practicing ending conversations strongly, practicing small talk, when and where you can acting like close friends with strangers having conversational goals with people.

Everything we've discussed in this chapter should have given you a thorough understanding of small talk, allowing you to become a master of it. As I previously stated, take the points and strategies that speak to you and apply them to your own life. Don't try to implement everything all at once because it will be overwhelming and unsustainable. Take one step at a time on your path to improvement.

We can now proceed to my favorite chapter.

Chapter 7

Intricate Ways to Be More Charismatic

"Charisma is a glimmer in people that money cannot buy." It's a form of energy that is invisible but has visible effects." -Marianne Williamson

What exactly does charisma mean to you?

Google defines charisma as the quality of personal magnetism and charm that you have most likely encountered several times in your life. Those are the people you listen to and can't help but think, Damn, this person is cool. I'd like to spend more time with this individual and learn more about what they have to offer.

I saw this "charm" all the time in the sales industry. I would go into client meetings and listen to companies pitching to us or us pitching to them, and some of the people I saw had you hanging on their every word from the moment they opened their mouths. They were simply exceptional public speakers. When they finished, it was as if I'd been jolted back into reality, and I was left wondering where I'd been for the previous hour.

Being in the presence of a charismatic person is more of an experience than a conversation.

Perhaps you've met a boy or girl in a bar and struck up a conversation with them, only to become engrossed in the experience of them simply being, well, them. Whatever length of time that experience lasts, you're always left wanting more. They leave an impression on you that you will never forget.

If you've seen television shows like Mad Men, Queen's Gambit, or even Friends, you'll know that charisma doesn't always come in the form of a big ego. It's not just men in suits who know their industry inside and out, or women in attractive dresses who act mysterious and subtle. That is far from the case. These are perhaps traditional views on charisma, but they are now out of date and barely relevant.

Charisma comes in all shapes and sizes, and even someone you might consider a "book nerd" can have a lot of charisma when talking about their favorite characters, plot lines, and endings. So, how do you access your own reservoir of charisma? How do you entice others and entice them to be drawn to you and the energy you have to offer the world?

This, like small talk and listening, is a skill that can be learned by grasping a few fundamental truths.

You're in charge of the situation.

What is it that charismatic people in your life have never been?

They most likely did at some point in their lives, but they were charismatic at the time, so what weren't they?

Let me give you a hint. It's the same feeling as when you're about to ride a roller coaster and have no idea what's going to happen. Is it going to be exciting or terrifying? Are you going to scream or shout? Are you planning to pee or throw up? If you do, God forbid you hit the kid behind you. If you can't tell, I'm not a huge fan of theme parks.

The characteristic is, of course, nervousness.

Charismatic people manage their nerves in such a way that they are confident and believe they are supposed to be a part of the interactions they are in. You will be nervous if you do not feel as if you belong. When you put too much pressure on the outcome of a situation, you'll feel nervous, which is ridiculous when you consider the reality of the situation.

Assume you're back in college and spot a boy or girl you like and want to ask them out.

If you're nervous, it means you're putting all of the weight of the conversation on what they say. You're not in the moment when someone's response (the outcome of the situation) becomes the most important part of the conversation. Remember how motivational quotes say that life is about the journey rather than the destination? The same reasoning applies here.

This means you're putting too much pressure on the outcome of the conversation. As a result, you'll believe you have to "act" perfectly in order to get what you want, which is, of course, impossible. Instead, by being present, actively listening, and simply conversing with this love interest with the goal of enjoying their company right now, it really doesn't matter whether they say yes or no to asking them out. Instead, the most important factor is the quality of your interaction.

When you're not focused on the outcome, there's less pressure, and you'll naturally be more charismatic and confident, so if you do ask the other person out, they'll be having a much more positive time than dealing with the nervous version of you, and are thus more likely to say yes.

To summarize, don't put yourself under too much pressure in social situations. Instead of focusing on the outcome or the "end goal," enjoy the interaction itself. You'll be less nervous and more charismatic as a result.

The importance of relatability

The subheading is self-explanatory. I remember going to a blood donor's session a few years ago, and after you donate blood, you have to wait ten minutes to make sure you don't pass out and everything goes smoothly. It's not all bad because you get a cup of tea and a biscuit.

Anyway, I was waiting in the post-donation room one time when a guy came in and sat next to me. I'm not sure how it happened, but we ended up talking about his swimming history, and how to be better at gliding through the water, and how to go faster and be more efficient, and then all the medals he won, and so on. With all of this talk about swimming, I'm beginning to think it's something I should start thinking about incorporating into my life.

Everything he said was fine, and some of it was actually quite interesting. Yes, as someone who makes a conscious effort to listen, I may have learned a thing or two, but there was a problem. I couldn't help but be uninterested in what he had to say because it was completely unrelated to me. I didn't swim and didn't care much about it. He seemed to be using me as a platform to brag about himself and his accomplishments, and I felt compelled to agree with everything he said.

That is not a two-way conversation, and it is extremely boring to me. Anyone would find it tedious.

Use this in your own interactions to make what you're saying more relatable to the person with whom you're conversing. The more you get to know someone, the easier it will be to do this. However, until you get to that point, try focusing on asking the right questions that will help you understand the other person better, allowing you to choose topics about which you can both talk.

Charismatic people include everyone and do not use conversations solely to promote themselves.

Remembering the Names of Others

"A person's name is the sweetest sound in the world to that person," says Dale Carnegie, one of the most popular and influential authors in sales training and interpersonal skills.

And it's correct. We all prefer to be addressed by our given names, and you should be aware of how awkward it can be when you're speaking with someone and can't recall their name for the life of you.

Being like this will not make someone feel special or allow them to positively relate to you. Taking the time to remember someone's name consciously and purposefully can make a huge difference in your relationships with them. It demonstrates that you care about and respect that person enough to get to know them properly. These are strong, charismatic characteristics. Here are some pointers to get you started:

Be present when speaking to the other person so you hear their name correctly. Repeat the person's name back to them to ensure you heard it correctly. Make an association (i.e., Harry with the round glasses). Make a rhyme out of their name.

Be witty.

I debated whether to include this section because, while being funny and humorous is an excellent way to connect with people, not everyone is funny in the same way, and we all find different things humorous. This may make it difficult to connect with others because if your sense of humor differs from someone else's, things may not go well.

Remember what we said about keeping offensive jokes to a minimum? It's difficult to be funny, especially in front of strangers.

That being said, a charismatic person will be able to read the room, choose the appropriate level of hilarity, and make it work. If you've discovered in the past that you're a naturally funny person, even if you're funny in your own unique way, embrace it when the opportunity arises.

Charisma and humor go hand in hand, and being able to put a smile on someone else's face is a priceless gift you should possess. If you believe you have the potential to be funny, here are some quick-fire tips to improve your conversational skills:

Watch comedy programs and live shows to get ideas for what's funny. Find and follow comedians you like. Learn three awesome jokes you like and perfect how to tell them.

Experiment with not being offended by other types of comedy.

Giving, Giving, Giving

This is another intriguing point to consider.

In an interview with Success.com, Eric Matthews of Start Co. stated that giving more than you take is one of the most beneficial ways to be charismatic in the business world, and this also applies to life in general. Being charismatic by nature means uplifting those around you and making their lives better in some way.

You can do this in simple ways, such as giving someone your full attention or complimenting them. You can validate and reassure them by repeating what they said.

There isn't a single person on the planet who doesn't want this kind of attention.

The real trick here is to first focus your attention on the other person. People will be much more willing to converse with you in depth if you do this.

Second, you can't expect anything in return. To some extent, this stinks because many conversations can feel one-sided, but here's a reminder that you don't always have to speak to that person again if they're not someone you want to spend time with and it doesn't become a two-way experience when you're with them. You don't have to befriend everyone, but that doesn't mean you can't be a charismatic person.

Here are a few pointers to help you be more clear:

Give genuine compliments if you mean them Give someone your undivided attention Don't expect anything in return Be polite and courteous Be open and honest with the other person (don't wear a mask)

The Synopsis

Being charismatic is a skill that must be developed over time and through practice.

Don't worry if you didn't get everything you came for in this chapter; it's just an introduction to things you can work on. Give these points some time, and you'll notice an immediate improvement in your charisma. In the following chapters, we'll go into greater detail.

For reference, the core values you'll want to keep in mind here are:

Remember that you belong in any situation. Be relatable to the people you're speaking with. Remember the names of the people you're speaking with. Allow humor to flow naturally.

For the time being, these should be enough little tips and tricks to keep you on your way to becoming a charismatic person who can speak to anyone. It won't be easy, and it will take some practice, but it will all come together in the end. Simply be aware of what you're doing and step out of your comfort zone to try new things!

This is the only way you'll be able to see the results!

Chapter 8

How to Be More Confident

"Confidence is the most beautiful thing you can wear." Blake Lively's

The ability to be confident goes hand in hand with charisma. You probably saw this coming, and believing you lack confidence was probably one of the reasons you picked up this book in the first place. If so, this is the chapter for you, but I'm hoping you can see how everything we've talked about already connects and will naturally help you become more confident, simply because you have more strategies to implement in your upcoming conversations.

Being charismatic and being confident are not the same thing, even though they complement each other perfectly.

Being charismatic, according to the dictionary, is having a charm that makes people want to be around you and spend time with you; being confident is having the belief that the outcome of a situation will be favorable to you. In other words, you can enter a conversation knowing that everything will be fine and that you will not be embarrassed or make a mistake, and even if you do, you will know that everything will be fine.

Remember what we discussed in the previous chapter about asking someone out on a date? If you're nervous and unconfident, you'll act nervous and unconfident, and the situation will become a self-fulfilling prophecy. On the other hand, if you're confident and present yourself well, your chances of getting a date skyrocket.

So, how do you go about it? Let us investigate.

Make it up until you make it.

You've probably heard this adage before, but science suggests that acting a certain way is one of the best ways to become a certain way. In other words, if you act confident, you will eventually become confident.

This is known as the Hebbian Principle in psychology and neuroscience. When a human does something, which can literally be anything, the tiny neural circuits in their brain light up and begin firing in order to make the "thing" happen. Assume you want to raise your right arm right now. You think about it, and those circuits begin to fire, sending signals to your body to lift your arm. You can try to avoid doing it if you really want, but how aware are you of your arm right now?

If you raise your arm, the message you sent becomes a "link," and the more you allow this link to occur, the easier it becomes.

The human brain prefers the simple life, which is why so many of us have habits. We've done the same habit so many times that we do it without thinking, so the brain saves energy and just "does," rather than thinking all the time.

Are you still with me?

We've progressed so far that you can actually trick this system into developing new habits, or in this case, entirely new states of mind, simply by thinking about doing something. Let's keep it on the topic of confidence.

If you wake up in the morning, go to the mirror, and act like your most confident self, portraying the level of confidence you want yourself to have, and actively acting out how you would be (yes, this includes talking to yourself out loud), you will naturally become more confident over time because you are firing up those circuits saying that you want to be more confident, and then carrying out that command.

Your brain is actively hardwiring. It's a brilliant technique.

This is why, before going on stage, motivational speakers will jump up and down and build up their energy. Tony Robbins, a well-known motivational speaker, has a mini-trampoline on which he jumps just before taking the stage. It's to boost his energy and get his blood flowing so that when it's time to perform, he's already in the high-energy state of mind he needs to be in.

You, too, can do the same!

Simply define the type of person you want to be and the level of confidence you want to have, practice it in your spare time, and then begin to naturally implement this level of confidence in your interactions, and you'll notice a huge difference! Here are a few pointers that helped me get through this process:

Watch movies and TV shows to see what kind of people you resonate with to define your confidence style; do the same with people in your life; practice in front of the mirror for five minutes every day; experiment with different confidence styles; and apply your practices to everyday situations you find yourself in.

Overcome Self-Sabotaging Thoughts

Limiting beliefs are thoughts that prevent you from living the life you want to live and hold you back, and they are crushing your confidence.

Assume you're going into a job interview and you're extremely nervous. You can't help but worry that you're going to screw everything up, and you keep running through all the possible outcomes of the meeting. How can you expect to be confident if you're only focusing on the negative? You're not going to be your best self today.

The solution to this problem is to become aware of your limiting beliefs. You can do this over time by journaling, meditation, counseling, and doing everything we discussed in the first chapter about developing your sense of self. But there is something we can do right now, and it's a fun little exercise that I enjoy.

A Quick Little Test

Take out a pen and paper and pretend you're meeting someone for the first time.

It could be a new client, a stranger in a cafe or on the street, or you're about to enter an unfamiliar situation in which you'll need to talk to people you don't know very well, if at all.

Take a moment to visualize it clearly, and then write down any negative thoughts that arise. Do you believe these people will find you strange or annoying? Are you concerned about your physical appearance? Are you concerned that they will dislike you or speak down to you? Make a list of everything that comes to mind.

When you read them back, you'll notice that these are your limiting beliefs, and you'll need to work on them if you want to become more confident. These are the kinds of thoughts that will hold you back from reaching your full potential. Of course, there are an infinite number of thoughts that could arise here, and it will take time to work through them all, but thankfully, there are a plethora of articles, books, and websites that can assist you in addressing your concerns.

For me, I was afraid that people would think I didn't know what I was talking about and that I wasn't qualified to share my experience because I was still young. However, after doing some research, I discovered that this is a mental state known as Imposter Syndrome, and I was able to take steps to work on letting go of these limiting thoughts.

While unrelated, I found this limiting beliefs discovery technique to be very enjoyable when it came to looking at your finances. Take out your pen and paper once more, and write down your ideal annual salary. Now, add a zero to the end (the right-hand side end) and list all of the reasons why you won't be able to earn that amount.

These are your limiting beliefs, and it's always fascinating to see what comes up!

Use Self-Assured Body Language

Amy Cuddy, a leading Harvard psychologist, investigated body language and how the way we act physically affects our mindset, state of mind, and overall confidence. In her research, she had 42 men and women perform what are known as low and high power poses.

These are basically poses that demonstrate how self-assured someone is. In other words, the stereotypical image of a shy person is hunched and crouched, as if trying to hide and not be noticed. A power pose that exudes confidence, on the other hand, would be similar to the Superman pose, with hands on hips and head held high.

Participants in the study were asked to hold certain poses for two minutes before saliva samples were taken.

The outcomes were unmistakable. People who adopted high-power poses, such as the Superman pose, had lower cortisol (the stress hormone) levels and higher testosterone levels, indicating that they were more relaxed, confident, less stressed, and more willing to rest. And it was all for the sake of striking a different pose.

You can feel the effects right now, which goes hand in hand with faking it until you make it. Assuming you're reading this while sitting, straighten your back and sit back with your hands behind your head, also known as the "President's Pose." It appears to be the classic office desk pose in which you've just finished a sale and cross your legs up on the desk because you're so pleased with what you've just accomplished, though having your legs on the desk is optional.

Pose with strength, widen your chest, and do a pose that makes you feel proud. Any stereotypical pose that comes to mind will suffice. Hold the pose for 30 to 60 seconds. What are your thoughts? How self-assured and ready to face the world does it make you feel? This demonstrates how powerful a seemingly insignificant act can be.

When you practice these poses in tense situations, you will become far more confident than you would normally be!

Get Your Hands On

Using your hands as your primary expressive form of body language can be a great way to feel, look, and become more confident. Carol Kinsey Gorman discovered that public speakers who exaggerate and communicate their points with their hands have a much more positive connection with their audience.

The same is true the other way around. Playing with your hair, fiddling with your sleeves or clothes, or sitting with your hands in between your legs can give the impression that you're nervous or anxious. Take control of your hands and direct your inner energy toward whatever topic you're discussing!

Implement Make Eye Contact

The ability to make and maintain eye contact is the foundation of confidence. When you look away from someone while they're talking to you, look at the ground, or anywhere other than you, it exudes a lack of confidence. When someone is embarrassed about something they've done, they look at the ground because they can't bear making eye contact. Even dogs engage in this behavior!

According to a 2013 Texan study, people make eye contact between 30 and 60% of the time on average, but if you want to make an emotional connection with someone, you'll need to increase this to 60–70% of the time. And it isn't easy.

If you're consciously considering making eye contact with someone for a longer-than-normal period of time, but it's not something you're used to, you're likely to feel uneasy and even as if you're staring. This will make you nervous, and your confidence will begin to crumble.

However, there are some pointers you can use to make it easier, and remember that practice makes perfect, so keep trying!

To begin, you do not need to lock your gaze on both of the other person's eyes; instead, focus on one. This may appear strange, but it works. If you're still uneasy, consider looking at their brows. Don't look higher or lower than their eye level because it will feel strange, as if you're not paying full attention. Eyebrows are in good shape. Improve your results by practicing in front of a mirror.

When you combine this tip with the others we've discussed throughout this book, you should find yourself naturally making eye contact more and more. Simply keep practicing, and the results will follow.

Reduce your speed.

When people are nervous, they tend to speak quickly, and this is especially true for those who are new to public speaking. The idea is that someone speaks as quickly as possible so that they can finish what they're saying quickly and then stop talking. This, however, is a clear indication that you are both nervous and anxious, not only displaying this to the other person but also validating your fears to yourself.

The straightforward solution is to slow down. Slow down the rate at which you speak consciously.

I'm not saying go monotone and drag everything out, but find a nice pace you're comfortable with (which you can practice in the mirror!), and then, when you're nervous and find yourself speeding up, mindfully slow yourself down. According to research, 190 words per minute is the ideal speaking speed for being comfortable and effectively conveying your message.

The Synopsis

For the time being, this should be enough confidence content for you to sink your teeth into in order to get a sense of how to become more confident in your conversations. Remember that if you look good, you'll feel good, so go into every situation from now on with the intention of controlling your self-image and portraying yourself as the person you want to be.

You'll naturally become this person, and that's who you'll be! It may appear to be simple, but it is. We overcomplicate things and put so much pressure on ourselves to be the best version of ourselves that we forget the power lies in the small choices we make that shape our reality.

I like Matt D'avella's perspective on this. Taking the smallest steps is usually what allows you to make the biggest leaps, so once you're able to knuckle down these small but powerful tactics, the bigger benefits will fall into place.

To be clear, the key points we discussed for you to remember when it comes to being a more confident version of yourself are as follows:

Act confidently in order to become confident!

Work on letting go of limiting beliefs; control your hand gestures; make eye contact; and slow down your speaking process.

Chapter 9

How to Tell Stories That Stick

"Within each of us is a natural-born storyteller just waiting to be unleashed." —Ronnie Moore.

We've been telling stories for as long as humans have been living in caves and painting on the walls. This is why thousands of new books are published each year and why the drawings on the walls of the pyramids recount events from the past. Humans love stories, and telling a good one is one of the best ways to connect with someone.

The small-talk topics we've already discussed are fantastic for breaking the ice, but the truth is that many of the people you'll meet in your life are people who want to engage and interact with interesting people. Small talk will only get you so far before people start looking for real substance in what you're saying to them. There will come a time when people will want to hear true stories.

But how can you tell someone a story that will captivate them and have them hanging on your every word if you live a fairly generic, typical, mundane life?

To begin, stop believing that your life is any of those things because it isn't. It only feels that way to you because you live it every day and see all the mundane aspects, such as brushing your teeth and walking into town.

The actual substance of your life is incredibly interesting because you are the only person in the world who has ever done what you've done, made the decisions you've made, and will be the only human in all of humanity to experience what you've experienced. I'm not going to get any more philosophical than that for the time being (I just love how mind-boggling that whole thought experiment is), but my point is that we all have interesting lives.

You're one of them.

The problem is that not everyone is born a storyteller, but as with all forms of communication, it is a skill that can be learned and practiced. If you do this, and you're able to tell stories about your life that hold people's attention and make them want to know more, you'll be able to talk to anyone about anything, which is why we're here.

Locating the Assailant Plotline

First and foremost.

You won't be able to tell stories if you don't have any. This refers to the ability to look into your own daily life and find stories that matter and can be retold in an engaging manner. I know, the first thing that comes to mind is that your life isn't all that interesting, at least not in comparison to other people's, right? Yes, it is. You might just have to do some digging.

Of course, there will be key moments in your life that will naturally become great stories. Everything is new and exciting the day you get married or go on your first date. Perhaps you take a vacation for your birthday and have a fantastic time. Perhaps you attended a protest or witnessed a global event. These are simple tales.

However, when it comes to extracting stories from your daily life, you may need to dig a little deeper at first.

"So, what do you do for a living?"

"I work as a manager in a supermarket."

Stop. Is that the most engaging, enthralling, and exciting way to present that information? It may not appear so, but this type of information can be woven into the foundations of a beautiful story. Please try again.

"So, what do you do for a living?"

"I work as a manager in a supermarket, but I sometimes feel like a detective." I had to follow a shady-looking guy around the store Mission Impossible-style the other day who looked like he was about to steal several cases of alcohol."

Damn, the creative juices are flowing now, and the listener is thinking, Wait a minute, a guy in the store stealing alcohol? What \happened? Did you manage to catch him? Did he make any attempts to steal anything? You've introduced conflict and a plot, as in all good stories. The listener is now interested in learning more.

See how you've taken the really common and boring question of "What do you do?" that you could hear literally anywhere from a networking meeting to a BBQ with mutual friends, and your response has suddenly drawn the attention of everyone around you? All it took were a few extra words and seconds of talking.

I want you to try it for yourself right now, out loud. I just met you and inquired as to what you do. Don't be concerned if this is your first attempt. I'm only here to write, and no one is here to pass judgment, so be inventive.

So, what are you going to do?

Layer your response with what you do and a story about something that happened to you. Something that occurred within the last month.

Anything that comes to mind. At this point, we're just practicing and trying to get those synapses to fire. The more you practice recalling stories, the better the stories that come up will be. Here are some pointers to help you spot interesting stories in your daily life.

Keep a diary or journal and write down anything interesting that comes to mind. You'll be surprised at how much you remember by the end of the day.

Practice gratitude and meditation; this is a great way to improve your focus as you go about your day.

Place yourself in intriguing situations. Take the scenic route to work. Speak with new people and see what happens. You never know what experiences await you.

Take notes on your phone about what happens and practice dramatizing it.

Creating a Story Collection

Okay, you don't have to write a memoir of short stories about your life, but having a few stories in the bank that you can use when responding to frequently asked questions can be a great idea because they'll be well-rehearsed (at least over time) and you'll have experience retelling them (even if it's just telling them back to yourself in the mirror at first).

Some ideas for topics for some of these mini-stories include:

Your job, profession, or occupation

Something that happened in the last week Any plans you have for the future Stories about your neighborhood

Stories about your interests

I watched a mediocre samurai movie last weekend, but the main character, a ninja, would meditate while working on his bonsai trees. I was so inspired by the entire scene that I purchased a bonsai growing kit and planted the seeds this week. I assumed you simply planted the seeds in the dirt and waited for them to sprout, but no. The instructions said to soak them in water for 48 hours before storing them in the fridge for two months. What's the crazy part? The seeds turned the water a deep, swamp-green color.

It was so green that I dropped it out of shock, and it stained my worktops. I'm still scrubbing it out today.

In reality, I'm just living my life and trying out a new hobby, but this is just a brief example of how you can take an everyday situation in your life and share it in a way that makes people pay attention. However, this story is not perfect in and of itself, but I'll explain why and how in the following section.

For the time being, keep coming up with your own story ideas! Let's give it another shot.

"Hey! It's time to get back to work. "How did your weekend go?"

"Yeah, it's not bad. "I sat and watched Netflix."

"Fun."

"Yup."

Woah.Wonderful story. Not in the least mundane. Let's try it again, but this time add a story element to it.

"Hey! Thank you for returning. "How did your weekend go?"

"My weekend went well, but it paled in comparison to Friday night." My cat went insane and began jumping on all the furniture, eventually becoming stuck on a cabinet. We had to use a stick to knock her down."

"Wait a minute, what?!"

As you can see, finding these small stories from your life leads to a much larger discussion. You're responding to general small-talk questions, but you're not giving boring answers that, let's face it, no one wants to hear. People want to converse. Yes.

We are social beings. But, while answering small-talk questions can be fun for a while, people really want more. Isn't that what you want out of your conversations?

So, how do you go about finding these fascinating stories in your life? After all, poking your cat with a stick from a cabinet is something you have to do, but to others, it could be comedy gold. How do you tell the difference between the mundane and the fascinating?

In all honesty, anything can be turned into a good story. It's the manner in which you tell it that will draw people in. The best way to determine this is to consider what you find interesting in a story. These are the stories you'll be most invested in.

Some questions to consider include:

- Do you enjoy silly stories about pets?

- Do you enjoy stories that are exciting, unbelievable, and prove that reality is stranger than fiction?
- Do you enjoy wholesome stories?
- Do you enjoy serious stories?
- Do you enjoy reading informative stories?
- Do you enjoy current-events stories?
- Do you enjoy sweet, romantic stories?

Whatever kind of story you like, this is the kind of story you'll be able to tell with the most energy and passion, so start paying attention. Furthermore, keep in mind that a good story will always have something relatable in it, which is the element with which we will connect the most.

This explains why people enjoy gossip, happy endings, and embarrassing situations. We've all been there, and we know what it's like, for better or worse, all of which adds to the power of these stories. We all enjoy stories that make us feel something.

What is the Best Way to Tell a Story?

Of course, there are an infinite number of ways to tell a story. You could tell a micro-story, like the ones in the examples above, or you could tell a full-fledged story. Consider sitting around a campfire and telling longer stories to one another. In any case, how do you tell a story that people will want to listen to?

Think about the Length

The length of your story will be determined by the circumstances of your situation. If you're chatting with someone in line, you don't want to ramble on and on, potentially holding them up and annoying them. If you're an anxious person, telling a longer story may give you more time to worry about the delivery of what you're saying. In this case, it is always preferable to stick to shorter stories until you are more confident.

Always adjust the length of your story based on the situation. You can change the length of your story by changing the amount of detail you provide. If you've already made small talk with the listener and found some common ground, try to include details that will specifically resonate with them.

Choosing the Correct Particulars

Personally, I believe that the 1:1:1 method is the most effective way to tell people short stories. Each '1' represents one of the following: one action, one-sentence summary, and one emotion.

A short story should include all of these in some way for the sake of brevity. It's not as intimidating as it appears at first.

Try to identify each element in the following stories.

Last week, I went on a date and promptly dropped my plate of food onto my lap. I didn't know what to do, so I just got up and left—such an embarrassing situation.

When I was crossing the street the other day, a taxi swung around the corner and nearly hit me. I was so terrified that I nearly pooped myself!

We had to restart from scratch after accidentally deleting the client project. We worked 16 hours a day for two weeks, but there's no better feeling than when it's done.

As you can see, the story is based on an action, the story is short and sweet, and there is an emotion that makes the story relatable in just two sentences. You can now expand on these stories as much as you want, adding details, jokes, more emotions, and so on, but it's all up to you and your personal storytelling style.

The trick to using the 1:1:1 method is to be able to summarize your story in one sentence and to begin near the end of your story's climax. Begin near the "grit" to provide as much information as possible in the shortest amount of time.

Imagine a story about a jailbreak taking place to help you remember this strategy. It makes no difference whether you describe what happens in a single sentence or write an entire book about it. The conclusion of the story is that the jailbreak occurred.

Adding to Your Stories

The 1:1:1 method is perhaps the simplest way to tell a good short story that people will want to listen to. Because you can add as much or as little detail as you want or need, those three factors are always a great foundation to build your story on (and work as a standalone).

Some people will make do with minor details, but others will want to hear more of what you have to say, so how do you keep the conversation going? You employ structure.

I'll list the elements that comprise a story structure, but you can add and adjust them as you see fit. This is the same process that Pixar uses when creating and writing their stories. Take note: this is the step-by-step guide they use when making their movies.

- Laying the groundwork

The story's setting is established. Characters are introduced here, and the world is built. Use this section only if it has an impact on the rest of the story.

Otherwise, you can easily skip this section the majority of the time.

- A brief introduction

Typically, the first section will introduce a character and their life, as well as their daily routine, and will build tension for the rest of the story.

Make this part as brief as possible so that you can move on to the exciting part.

- Create a conflict.

A major event occurs, disrupting the normal flow of life and throwing a wrench in the works. Make certain that you include the emotion of what occurs here. Everything flips upside down at this point.

- The ramifications of conflict

What impact has the conflict and change had on everything? What are the ramifications of the occurrence?

- Additional ramifications

Add more consequences if necessary to emphasize what is happening and the magnitude of the event. You can skip this section, but two conflicts are usually ideal.

- ADDITIONAL IMPLICATIONS

With even more conflict, you can really drive home your points. (I'll show you how this works in the example below.) The more emotional resonance you have in the last three stages, the more emotionally attached your listener will be to your story!

- In conclusion,

In the story, what does the main character do to deal with or resolve the conflict? What steps must be taken? What problem must be solved, and how does this occur? Determine how the story is resolved.

- Aftereffects

What happened after the conflict was resolved and everyone was able to move on? There's more emotion here. Is it a better or worse conclusion? How has the event affected the characters?

This is a lot to take in, but don't let it overwhelm you. If something happens in your life that you want to remember and think would make a good story, take the time to remember the details.

Later, you can modify and expand your story to fit this structure. If you want to keep things simple, remember the general structure of what happened and tell it in chronological order.

I understand that all of this may seem overwhelming at first, and you may even be thinking that this isn't how great stories are told.

It's a lot of behind-the-scenes work, but when you think about motivational speakers and stand-up comedians, this is exactly the level of effort they put into their stories that makes them so successful.

Sure, you may not want to go all the way with the structuring and so on, but at least you have this knowledge to work with and understand how everything works. Let's say something happens, and you know it'll make a good story to tell others. You might want to think about how you're incorporating emotions into your story, or how you're emphasizing the conflict of what happened, and so on. Your stories will only get better with practice and experience.

Finally, all of this is done to allow you to share your stories more naturally while still understanding where to apply details in the appropriate places.

Here's an example story that demonstrates how this structure works.

I was driving to work along the main road, you know the ones with the trees and fields on either side? I was following this lorry, and there was a car in front of me with its hazard lights turned on, parked on the side of the road. I slowed down, and this dog bolted into the road.

The truck swerved to miss it by such a small margin that it jumped the ditch and ran into the woods. The truck continued on, and I pulled over to the side of the road. The woman in the front seat was crying her eyes out, having a panic attack because her dog had jumped out the window while she was driving, and she couldn't get it back in. It kept coming back, running across the road and then back, as if it was playing a game.

I stayed with her for a half-hour while another car pulled over and the man inside offered assistance. We walked through the woods until we were able to capture the dog and return it to its owner, who burst out laughing. It was such a touching moment. She vowed she'd never drive again with her windows all the way down.

By the way, this is a true story.

This is a casual story written in the way you'd say it out loud, perhaps in response to "Why are you late for work?" It's a little long and can be refined to become more comprehensive. Here's an edited version that emphasizes the structure.

(Introduction) I was driving down a country road when I noticed a car parked ahead with its hazard lights flashing. (Conflict) As I slowed down to see if I could assist, a dog darted out into the road, directly in front of an oncoming truck (Consequence). Thank goodness it missed it, but only by a hair's breadth.

When the truck swerved, the dog leapt into the ditch and ran back into the woods. (As a result, I pulled over and noticed the woman in the parked car.) She told me, through tears, that she was having a panic attack (consequence) because her dog had jumped out the window while she was driving and she couldn't get it to come back in. It continued to run across the road and then back into the woods, believing it was playing a game.

I stayed for a half-hour while another driver and I arrived to assist. We walked through the woods until we were able to capture the dog and return it to its owner. (Resolution/Conclusion) It was amazing to see her face light up. She vowed she'd never drive again with her windows all the way down. (Aftermath) Now, you're probably not going to have enough time to think and edit your story as you say it in a real-life conversation, which is why I recommend taking some time to familiarize yourself with this structure on your own time. You don't have to do this for every important story; just the ones that matter.

The goal is to become acquainted with these skills and this structure of storytelling, which all come with practice and an understanding of how it all works. I've lost track of how many hours I've spent in front of the mirror or cleaning up my house, just talking to myself and experimenting with the best way to tell this story to someone.

However, the benefits of this practice and behind-the-scenes work have always paid off when I'm around the water cooler and everyone is hanging on every word I say.

The Synopsis

Be mindful of the events and situations you find yourself in and be aware of them in your life. They can be the most mundane of experiences, but how you tell the story (and how much energy you put into it) is everything and determines whether you are a great, charismatic, and confident storyteller.

When you come across a story in your life that you want to keep, work on organizing the structure, identifying the various elements that make the story great, and you'll be able to bring them all together to tell a story about your everyday life that will captivate and wow whoever you're speaking to.

Putting all of this together, you should now be able to create compelling stories about events in your life, not only selecting good story ideas but also telling your stories in creative, captivating ways that will astound your listeners.

Chapter 10

Becoming an Interesting Person

"Your life is a canvas, and you are the artist." There are a million different ways to be kind, amazing, fabulous, creative, daring, and interesting." -Kerli's

When my social anxiety was at its peak, I was about 22 years old, and it seemed like my life consisted of nothing more than going to work, coming home, and playing video games.

I wasn't doing anything, I wasn't having new experiences, and I certainly wasn't creating memories that would last a lifetime.

While we discussed in the previous chapter how you can make stories sound interesting regardless of what is going on in your life, there is no doubt that you can be proactive in making your life more interesting by changing a few simple things. The thing is, doing more with your life will not only make you more interesting to talk to because you'll have more to talk about, but you'll also be happier with yourself and your life. As a result, you'll be more self-assured, charismatic, and authentic.

Come on, be truthful. Raise your hand if you've ever found yourself stuck in bad habits that don't add value to your life? Maybe you binge on entertainment, haven't created anything in a long time, or you have dreams of doing something, starting something, or going somewhere, but you keep putting it off for no apparent reason.

For many years, this was my relationship with writing.

I've always wanted to write books since I was a kid. I liked the idea of writing, and throughout my early twenties, I would write here and there, but I never made it a habit. I'd go weeks, then months, without writing anything, and it never really progressed. I couldn't tell people I write or want to be a writer if I wasn't writing, so something had to change.

This chapter will be devoted to sharing some tips and advice that I found useful in becoming a more interesting person and, ultimately, leading a more fulfilling life. In the most literal sense, this isn't for anyone but yourself, but there's no doubt that doing more interesting things, or at least becoming more aware and educated about more things in life, will help you connect more easily with others.

Just a quick note: I'm not saying you should do more with your life. This chapter is more concerned with helping you realize what is important to you, what fuels your sense of self (see chapter one), and then giving you the intention to cut out everything else that doesn't actually serve you or add value to your existence.

Okay, I'm sure you see where I'm going with this. Let's get started with the advice.

More Books to Read

To get us started, here's a really simple tip. How many books do you have at home that you've been meaning to read but haven't gotten around to it yet, nor do you have any firm plans to begin? That's all of me. My hobby is simply purchasing new books that I never read.

Reading is such an amazing pastime because it not only allows you to get lost in other worlds and the lives of fictional characters, but it also opens the door to more opportunities than you can imagine.

For example, I recently finished Blake Crouch's Dark Matter (which I highly recommend), which discusses Multiverse theory and quantum mechanics.

The story is incredible and one of my favorite books in a long time (I read it all in one sitting), but I was also curious about quantum mechanics. Now, I'm not sure how it all works, but I went down the rabbit hole and ended up discussing it all with someone at work who had a similar interest.

This opportunity arose as a result of my reading. I wouldn't be able to connect with my colleague in a new, interesting, and meaningful way if I hadn't read the books. You never know what opportunities await you around the next corner. Some reading tips include: locating some books that you enjoy. Whether it's fiction or nonfiction. Make a stack of them and go through the list.

Try books you would never normally read just to see how they are.

Find books that interest you and inspire, educate, and motivate you to try and explore new things in life.

If you need any more convincing to start a reading habit, there is a plethora of research that shows that reading trains your brain to be better at processing information. It also lowers your risk of age-related cognitive decline, lowers your risk of conditions like dementia (as demonstrated by a large 14-year study and another 2018 study on 16,000 people in China), reduces stress, and helps you live longer.

Change Up Your Routine

One of the best and simplest changes I've made in the last two years is to set my alarm much earlier than usual, so I can get up at silly o'clock in the morning (usually around 5 a.m.) and walk to the highest point in my city to watch the sunrise. It's a strange little ritual I perform once a month or so, and it truly brings me joy.

Changing up your routine and doing things "just because" is a great way to keep you on your toes and your life interesting.

When it comes to conversations, I can share my experiences (and sometimes I take the people I'm talking to with me the next time I go, and we enjoy it together). It creates interesting experiences that break up the monotony of everyday life, which we all fall victim to from time to time.

Furthermore, when you go on an unplanned whim, you never know what other experiences you'll have. I saw a group of baby foxes rummaging through bins the last time I went on the hike, and it was such a beautiful sight. I would have missed everything if I had stayed in bed.

Contribute Your Time

Volunteering your time benefits everyone involved.

Not only are you devoting some of your time to helping others and actually benefiting the communities or causes you're working for, but you're also becoming more interesting as a result of the experiences you're gaining.

In 2020, my partner and I volunteered at a cat shelter for a few months. It wasn't the best experience because I spent most of my time cleaning out cages and washing some of the cats, but it was fascinating to see how the cats come in, what the process is for dealing with and rehoming cats, and just how difficult and difficult it can be for both humans and animals.

It's all a learning experience, and if you're willing to let it in, it can bring so much into your life.

Accept Your Fear

This is a practical tip that you can put to use right away. Do you get that little pang in your stomach when you go to do something new or enter an experience you're not sure about? That feeling that you don't know how to proceed? Take note of that sensation and try to move through it. Accept your fear and don't let it hold you back.

In an interview, Will Smith famously stated, "Everything good in life can be found on the other side of fear." All you have to do is take a leap of faith in yourself. Remember that your fear of being uninteresting causes you to be uninteresting. These emotions suffocate you and keep you trapped, rather than allowing you to live freely.

Use Your Time Wisely

It's well known that the only real resource you'll ever have to invest in your life is your time. Even if you work, you are essentially exchanging your time for money. While there are things we must do in order to survive, it can be a game changer when you really start to see where your time is going.

Do you spend all of your time watching television? Have you been scrolling through your social media feeds?

Visiting the same vacation spots year after year? Every weekend, you're drinking and partying? Sure, if you're doing something you enjoy, you should keep doing it. That's all right.

However, this is not the case for all of us, and many of us are faced with the very real realization that we are most likely wasting our lives. If you want to be interesting and feel like you can get more out of life, start thinking of your time as a currency and pay attention to where you spend it.

Have Interesting Discussions

If you ask someone how they are but don't care about the answer, this will come out like a house on fire.

Lazy, uninterested people stick to small-talk topics like the weather and asking if they're watching any good TV shows (remember that most TV is just a passive activity that won't really bring you any benefit), or asking what you do for a living. BORING! It's fine once in a while and when you're first starting out, but after everything you've read so far, you're clearly past this point.

Instead of boring topics, ask what personal projects someone is working on, what the strangest thing they have ever eaten, what items are on their bucket list, or if they are learning any new skills.

Finding answers to these questions can open up whole new worlds to you that you were previously unaware of. You never know when you'll be introduced to something new that you'll fall in love with, or when you'll learn something new that will change your life.

Attempt New Hobbies

This doesn't really require much explanation, so I'll keep it brief.

I sat down at the start of 2020 and wrote down everything I actually care about. I had fun writing. I was interested in spiritual concepts such as meditating and lucid dreaming. I wanted to improve my French skills. I wanted to learn the proper way to play chess. I wished I had more time to read. I wanted to learn to play blues guitar.

This was just me sitting down to make a list of all the hobbies I wanted to pursue.

Take a pen and paper and jot down everything you're interested in and want to get involved in right now. Even if you've never given the activity or hobby much thought before and it's more of a passing thought, write it down.

These are all the things you care about, and you know you do because you wrote them down! Determine which hobbies you enjoy the most and which you want to get involved in. Make time for them and enjoy the experience of doing so! You will not only meet new people, but you will also have interesting topics to discuss with others!

The Synopsis

There are countless ways to be proactive and become a more interesting person, giving you more to talk about and making you happier with the way you spend your time. Everyone has the potential to be more interesting. It's simply a matter of taking action on your own.

Sure, you may simply need to work on breaking out of some bad habits, replacing them with good ones, and overcoming the fear that's holding you back, but this is where you must be patient and believe in the long run. Remember that small steps can lead to big leaps.

ChapterEleven – Creating Meaningful Relationships

"Each friend represents a world in us, a world that may not have been born until they arrived, and it is only through this meeting that a new world is born." -Anais Nin's

And now we're here. We've arrived at the end of the book. As you can see, the final title of this book is "Developing Meaningful Relationships," but we've spent the majority of our time so far on conversations and being able to talk to anyone about anything, which you should be able to do by now. However, the final question is straightforward.

How do you go from knowing someone and impressing them with your charm, confidence, and small talk to developing a proper relationship with them? How do you meet people and make genuine friends with them?

It's strange to think that so many of us are becoming increasingly disconnected in a world that is more hyper-connected than ever before. I can't remember exactly, but it seemed like making friends was so simple when I was a kid in school. Sure, you wouldn't get along with or enjoy the company of everyone (that would be strange), but there were no reservations about meeting new people. You'd just talk about whatever was on your mind, and if you got along, you'd become friends.

It appears that there is an underlying level of pressure and anxiety that prevents things from being that simple today. It's a cringe-worthy thought to imagine approaching someone and simply talking to them, only to become lifelong friends. Perhaps in an ideal world, right? Perhaps you believe logic only works in movies. It isn't. It only takes a little time and effort to see what life could be like in a different way.

Taking everything you've learned thus far, how can you progress from meeting someone for the first time, small-talking with them, telling them stories, charming them with your charisma and confidence, and eventually becoming friends with them, or at the very least developing a meaningful relationship of some kind?

This chapter will show you exactly how.

The Advantages are Unrivaled

While having strong connections with people in your life and talking to many people will make you feel less lonely and more charismatic and confident, having a million acquaintances is no substitute for having five friends with whom you have a deep and meaningful connection.

According to research, having proper connections with people can bring so many benefits into your life that it's difficult to know where to begin. According to a 2014 study conducted by the Society for Personality and Social Psychology, meaningful relationships will: help you live longer, improve many aspects of your mental health, improve your ability to judge your own well-being increase your self-confidence, provide you with broad perspectives, provide you with increased resilience in most aspects of your life.

According to some sources, having meaningful relationships is "the healthiest thing you can do for yourself" (Medical Daily, 2014). In other words, prioritize the formation of meaningful relationships. This will bring a lot of good into your life.

Understanding the Obstacles

To fully comprehend how to make close friends, you must first understand what is preventing you from doing so. The two main culprits are: Having a busy life, such as working full-time jobs, working on side projects, and trying to keep up with the fast-paced life that feels common, as promoted by the "mainstream" way of life.

In other words, just because your best friend's name appears in your Facebook feed doesn't mean you're connecting with them. You need to put down your phone and properly reach out to them, as well as make time to have actual experiences with them, but more on that later.

Now we'll look at how to take these early relationships in your life and move forward, forming stronger bonds than ever before and connecting with the people you might one day say you love.

You Can't Be Friends With Everyone

Before we get into the tips, make sure you're aware that you won't be friends with everyone, and you shouldn't try to be.

I'm not suggesting that you be rude and forceful to people you don't like. Maintain civility. Instead, if you have a natural attraction to someone and feel a connection, it's something you should definitely pursue. It doesn't matter if you don't. You're one step closer to meeting the people who are right for you.

Spend Time with Your New Companions

As I write this book, the world is gripped by the COVID-19 pandemic, which has thrown everything into disarray in ways we could never have predicted. Many of us have become more disconnected as a result of lockdown rules, but the happiest people were those who still found a way to connect and spend time together.

If you want to connect with someone and deepen your relationship with them, you must spend time with them, make memories together, and be physically present in each other's presence, not just online. It's clear that in times like the COVID-19 pandemic, connecting in such an intimate way isn't always possible, but that doesn't make spending time with each other any less important.

Spending time with people is essential whether you're going for a socially distant walk, hosting online activities like Zoom quiz nights or group Netflix streams, or simply chatting via video call.

Relationships grow by devoting time to each other (while ensuring that it is equitable both ways).

Support One Another

According to new research, friends become closer than ever when they help one another through difficult times. This could be anything from offering support on a friend's self-improvement journey to dealing with a tragedy or trauma. Going through change with someone by your side is always easier and more effective.

In a 2008 study, researchers assigned some participants to stand at the top of a hill alone, alongside a stranger, or next to a friend.

When asked to grade how steep the hill was, those standing next to a friend thought it was far less steep than those standing alone. In other words, when you're standing with someone you care about, the bad times don't seem so bad.

Be True to Yourself

Finally, and perhaps most importantly, be yourself in front of those you care about.

It can be difficult to admit we're wearing masks around those we care about, let alone try to remove them, but it's never been more important to embrace who you are and just be yourself.

If you pretend to be someone you're not with your friends, it will eventually backfire. Either you won't be happy or your friends won't be happy, so save yourself the drama and just be yourself. Even if you change over time (as everyone does), true friends will accept you for who you are.

That's it! If you can master these simple tricks and tips, you'll be able to transform the people you know and like in your life into friends with whom you share a deep, meaningful connection, and the world will become your oyster.

The Synopsis

Relationships are essential. Take everything you've learned in this book and simply jump from person to person, attracting them with your charm, hooking them with your stories, and becoming such a memorable person in their lives, but then move on without developing deeper relationships with people along the way. You'll feel lonely and unsatisfied with your life.

Take the time to invest in your relationships. You can choose who you want to be friends with, but it's important to give people a chance. As someone who has struggled with social anxiety for many years, I understand how difficult and frightening it can be to open up to others, but trust me when I say it will be one of the best things you ever do.

To summarize, some of the elements you should pay attention to are: Understanding what holds you back, remembering that you can't be friends with everyone, spending time with one another,being yourself!

It's time to say good-bye!

Last Thoughts

So, we've reached the end of our journey, and it's all up to you!

I hope you've enjoyed reading this as much as I have, and that you've learned a lot. I know I said it a few chapters ago, but here it is again for good measure: Don't give up on your learning path! Like all self-improvement journeys, the path to better communication is a never-ending learning curve with an infinite skill cap. You can always get better and better at it.

However, the only way to do this is to practice over and over, being willing to embrace any fears or anxieties you may have in order to overcome them. Just keep at it, take everything we've discussed in baby steps, and you'll see huge improvements in no time!

I'm just a regular person doing what I enjoy, but I'm always striving to improve and provide you with the best experience possible! I'd also love to hear about all the amazing ways these books have changed your perspective on life, so please share and inspire me to keep going!

CPSIA information can be obtained
at www.ICGtesting.com
Printed in the USA
LVHW080738060422
715401LV00010B/434